Muir and More

Ronald Turnbull

MUIR AND MORE
John Muir, his life and walks

Drawings by Colin Brash

Millrace

First published in Great Britain in 2008 by
Millrace
2a Leafield Road, Disley
Cheshire SK12 2JF
www.millracebooks.co.uk

ISBN: 978-1-902173-27-6

Typeset in Adobe Garamond Pro
Printed and bound in the United Kingdom
by T J International Ltd, Padstow, Cornwall PL28 8RW

John Muir
1838–1914

The John Muir Trail
Yosemite Valley to Mount Whitney
210 miles

The John Muir Way
Dunbar to Fisherrow
45 miles

Dedication

Like John Muir, we found a warm welcome in the United States. *Muir and More* is dedicated to 'Primrose' and 'Chanson', Jim from Georgia, and all the companions of the John Muir Trail; and to the Ford family of North Carolina.

Contents

Maps

The first wild creature we saw, out of the bus window as we approached the Sierra Nevada, was the American red-tailed hawk. It was soaring to lift the heart above some scrubby yellow grassland.

The red-tail hunts from the sky or from a high perch. It dives at 120mph, but walks awkwardly. The wingspan is about four feet. In the mating season, or when annoyed, it screams rather like an old-fashioned steam train. One recording of a red-tail has been used and reused to add atmosphere to many different Western movies, and as a 'soundtrack double' for the rather wimpy noise of a bald-headed eagle.

The red-tail has eyesight eight times as sharp as us humans, and has been around for five times as long. It is territorial, and monogamous—at least when living in the countryside. 'Pale Male', who lives on an apartment building in New York just across the road from Woody Allen, has had four mates; but has been described as a 'cool dad' because of his parental involvement in fledgling flying lessons. Red-tails eat voles and mice mostly, but anything from beetles to jackrabbits, and as vermin control are helpful to humans. Meanwhile, humans' habit of building electricity poles above open road verges, and woodlots in alternation with open pasture, is helpful to the red-tailed hawk.

There's nothing rare or special about the red-tail: it occurs a million strong all over the USA. Sitting on the stoop with your honey lamb and watching it 'makin' lazy circles in the sky': this is a fundamental act linking an American and his landscape—at least according to Oscar Hammerstein II (Oklahoma! 1943).

John Muir hunted down eagle feathers to make his quill pens. But in this book, chapters are headed by the red-tailed hawk.

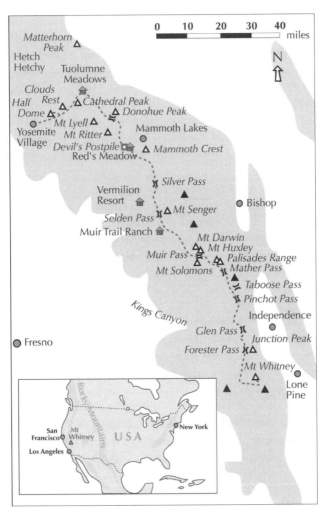

The John Muir Trail, Sierra Nevada, California

Introduction

One day's exposure to mountains is better than cartloads of books.

John Muir

 Every game has its homeland. Walking up pretty hills and going to the pub: you can do it in various parts of the world, but England's Lakeland is where it's all about. My personal game of austere hikes with bivvy-bag is basically Highland Scotland. Mountaineering—rocky ridges, snowy crests, glaciers —happens in the Alps and is referred to in several languages as 'Alpinism'. Nepal is the spiritual centre of yakpacking—hand your luggage to a helpful inhabitant who also boils the evening lentils, get altitude sickness, use up a lot of photo film and not that much boot sole.

What St Andrews is to golf, North America is to backpacking. Country where you walk for 250 miles without crossing a road; where you get attacked by biting insects but also by bears; where you camp for five days while a river runs down after a storm. And so we get the frightful ergonomics of how to don a 50lb rucksack: that being an act I set off from Yosemite sincerely hoping not to have to perform. In navigation, the technique of 'aiming-off' is applied over a fortnight of empty country, eventually arriving at the handrail road just 40 miles from the intended target.

And yet, like golf itself, like deerstalking, backpacking seems to have been invented by a Scotsman. 'I only took a walk in the Yosemite,' says Johnnie Muir from Dunbar, 'but stayed for six years.' America invites excess, and Americans do tend to overdo things. Even so, Muir's followers along the Pacific Crest and Appalachian Trails spend a mere six months afoot before retiring to some cosy city to replace their equipment, relearn their social skills, and earn a little money for the next hiking season.

So to call the John Muir Trail, in California's Sierra Nevada, the best long walk in the world is wrong straight away. By the standards of the country, and of the man who gave it his name, it's a short saunter that, even if you embrace that unnecessarily heavy backpack, still takes a mere three weeks. Cricket is the best game in the world—if you happen to like cricket. Long or not, the John Muir Trail is the best walk in the world—if what you like is a self-reliant journey through remote country inhabited by bears.

If what you like is a mule path through the wilderness and being a beast of burden yourself as you hoof along it. If what you like is big trees and bare granite. If what you like is …

… a wide, well-built path that after five days heads gradually down to the outflow of a narrow lake. The slopes around the lake are tumbled boulders and ice-smoothed granite slabs, but the path is terraced across the stone-fields and carved into the occasional outcrop. The tree roots tangle in a maze of boulders, and their trunks and branches above are twisted in sympathy.

Beyond the lake rises a tall, shapely mountain. On our map it has no name, and some of its buttresses might even be unclimbed, for we are several days away from the nearest car-parks. Half-way through a September afternoon, me and Tom may be the only people looking at this particular mountain and this particular lake.

The lake we look at is blue-grey; the sky above is grey with patches of gangrene yellow. Small thunderstorms are rumbling among the summits. We cross the outflow, and emerge from the lake's hanging valley to a hollow of dark forests. Ten miles away, the opposite slopes are mottled with scrub, then rise to slabs and domes of bare granite.

We descend in zigzags to a trail that contours along the valley. Between thick trunks we glimpse again the forest hollow below us. By late afternoon, the trail is descending again, to the outflow of Purple Lake. A single angler stands on the opposite shore. We drop the packs onto the strip of meadow between the lakeside and the rising trees. We stand for a minute. We wiggle our shoulder blades, let the power of thinking seep back into tired minds.

Just as we've got the tent up, it rains. It rains for twenty minutes; while I lie and listen to it on the green nylon, Thomas stands outside to see if he's going to get wet. The sun comes out, and we pour boiling water onto our dehydrated supper. Above the Purple Lake, buttresses of black basalt interrupt the granite hillside. As the sun sinks, the paler rocks turn golden. By the time we've finished eating, the forest is slaty grey, the granite rocks are delicate greyish pink.

The fishermen are apologetic. 'It doesn't normally do this, not at this time of year.'

They didn't really need to be embarrassed. Never, in my life so far, have I walked six days with only twenty minutes' rain.

'You see, we're from Scotland.'

'Oh, but John Muir was from Scotland!'

John Muir in bivvy

He was indeed; and, a century after his death, Scotland is starting to wake up to the fact. The Loch Lomond National Park has wandered through the

Sierra Club website, clipping sweetly-scented Muir quotes for its brochures and signage. Nineteen of his words have been carved into the new Scottish Parliament building in Edinburgh. But never mind the words: his walks have been commemorated with a 45-mile 'John Muir Way' along the bleak East Lothian coastline where he fell into the rock pools as a boy. In his name also, Schiehallion, Blaven and Ben Nevis have been purchased for wildlife and the people.

After we'd finished talking about bears, one of the American walkers kindly told us all about John Muir.

Notes and references

Unattributed Muir quotations throughout this book are mostly from his letters, and can sometimes be tracked down by an electronic search of the John Muir Exhibit on the Sierra Club's website.

p1 (epigraph) John Muir: 'Mountain Thoughts', written during the 1870s, collected by Linnie Marsh Wolfe and published in *John of the Mountains* (University of Wisconsin Press, 1981).

p2 ('I only took a walk') John Muir. Like many Muir quotes, this has been quoted and requoted by outdoor writers for a 100 years. It is surely authentic, but my attempt to trace the original has failed.

1 The John Muir Way: Towards Dunbar

*Beautiful hills and dales, green fields in the very
height of cultivation, and many belts and blocks
of woods so arranged as to appear natural. ... The
weather here reminds me of Alaska, cold and damp.*

John Muir

A windy night, in December 2007, on the
east coast of Scotland. Away to my right
a road rose over a rise, and car headlights
fanned across the night sky. Away on the
left, the nuclear power station three miles
away sent a wash of yellow sodium light over the top
of the grass bank. Although I was below the cliff rim,
the rumble and screech of the A1 road drifted over
my head as I slept. And my nose was hinting that
somewhere, some dog had disobeyed the Scottish
Parliament's new poop-scoop injunctions.

The price we pay for our comfortable, pleasant
life in the 21st century is this: a layer of ugliness
smeared over our entire countryside. An aeroplane
flashed its way like some night insect across the field
of stars. Blackness ahead was the Firth of Forth. At
midnight its muddy waters came across the flats and

almost drowned the noise of the dual carriageway.

I rose in cold darkness, and spooned in some cold muesli with, as a treat, a pint of fresh milk I'd carried from Cockburnspath. The path took me across a grey beach to Torness power station.

The orange glare of the high windows, and the softer pinkish glow of the concrete walls—all rising from a sparkly sea of little streetlights. Just two men sitting somewhere behind one of the high walls, watching a screen as every 100 seconds a fuel pellet drops like a pea into the machine, and keeping an eye on one another to make sure they don't fall asleep. Or perhaps there are 300 men in there in black uniforms with machine guns and anti-tank rockets, waiting through another night for the first ever terrorist attack on a working nuclear installation. Do they leave the sodium lights on all night as a display of its rigid, unceasing power output, or is it a sort of artwork, an attempt to express the alien and alarming beauty of nuclear fission reactions?

Last time I'd been here, I was in the mud in front of the bulldozers trying to prevent the place from ever existing at all. It was fun climbing into the buckets of the big digger machines. Nowadays, it's more complicated. Would you rather see a big dangerous place like Torness Power Station, or a line of wind turbines, just slightly less tall than the Yosemite sequoias, all along the Lammermuirs where John Muir used to run wild? Fortunately we don't have to make that difficult decision. Against global warming, both turbines and atom-plant are going to be necessary. These will be the 21st century's stratum of ugliness laid down across the damaged land. And the one dark part of my night landscape, the noisy sea, will become an offshore wind farm, and transform this winter wind into computer screens and low-energy light bulbs.

A concrete walkway leads around the power station. It's protected from the sea by a slope of several thousand abandoned trig points. The interpretation boards identify them as 'dolos blocks', a South African invention. The concrete pillar we see is just the corner of a twisted H-shape, designed so that the waves will only entangle them further. The assembly does not block the incoming wave, but breaks it up: the result is many times more resistant than a line of square stone blocks. The Afrikaans *dolosse* refers to knuckle-bones of goats or oxen, used in children's games and traditional fortune-telling: *Wat speel julle met die dolos?* (English: What are you playing at with the dolos?) This could be, after *trek*, the second Afrikaans word to enter English (*trek* is related to German *tragen*, to pull or carry, and English 'drag').

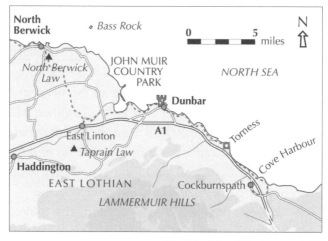

The John Muir Way (eastern half)

We need more, from the vigorous language that refers to a jeep's gearbox as *rattelkaas*.

An early use of the dolos blocks was at Durban. From there it's a simple transposition of letters to their use here at Dunbar. The sea wall is said by the interpretation board to be proof against a 10,000-year storm. As its concrete gives way to sea shingle, there appears around the next headland the floodlit chimneys of the Dunbar cement works that will be the next of the walk's ugly-building way markers.

One and a half centuries ago, industrial intrusion was a pair of flickering oil lamps on the front of a coach, its unoiled wooden wheels audible at a quarter of a mile. Even then, an unusually far-sighted man might realise that ever-cosier modern lifestyles, and our wild natural landscape, were not finally compatible. That unusually far-sighted man was born in 1838, just beyond the big cement works, in the red sandstone town of Dunbar. His name, which is also the name of the path I was walking along: John Muir.

If you want your offspring to grow into a really interesting person, one way is to give them a really interesting name—Tallulah Bankhead, or Oliver Wendell Holmes, or Theodore Roosevelt. But by the time Daniel Muir had that one worked out, the kid was called John and that was that. The other way, though, is a really interesting and unusual childhood. John Muir's childhood was interesting and unusual. Some of it was also enjoyable. The playground fights between streeties and shories—town kids and kids from the fishing community. The running wild in the Lammermuir Hills. The Dunbar shoreline with the dulse seaweed and the rock pools and the Bass Rock against the silver skyline. Muir loved

to gaze and wonder at the shells and seaweeds, eels

and crabs in the pools among the rocks when the tide was low; and best of all to watch the waves in awful storms thundering on the black headlands and craggy ruins of the old Dunbar Castle.

Some of it, on the other hand, was not enjoyable. The silent mealtimes. The nightly beatings. The backup beatings from the village schoolmaster. The reading and learning by heart of the whole of the New Testament and 75 per cent of the Old. (The 25 per cent left out would include the 'Song of Solomon', which is lyrical and slightly sexy.) The not reading of anything else at all.

Thirty years later, John Muir had a wild time on Mount Shasta, an ice-covered volcano only slightly lower than Mount Whitney and, being 300 miles further north, a much more serious mountain. Trapped on the summit in a blizzard, in his shirtsleeves, Muir spent the night warming himself at a volcanic fumarole. He wrote what was presumably a self-deprecating letter about his discomforts and the tough job of being a pretty successful outdoor writer. His Dad's reply has survived.

'If it had not been for God's boundless mercy you would have been cut off in the midst of your folly.' Daniel Muir doesn't say so, but one gets the impression that God's judgement and mercy wouldn't have been

Daniel's, if it had been Daniel deciding life or death on Mount Shasta, God sitting at home in Wisconsin and getting the letter about it afterwards. As for the outdoor writing: 'And the best and soonest way of getting quit of the writing and publishing your book is to burn it, and then it will do no more harm either to you or others.'

Dunbar is a handsome town built of Old Red Sandstone with pantiled roofs. In its high street, a bronze boy Muir gazes rapturously upwards at the Christmas lights. Muir is East Lothian's man of the millennium; East Lothian's John Muir Way is in direct competition with the same-named Trail in California's Sierra Nevada.

On a Tuesday morning in December, I'd expected the Muir Birthplace cottage to be bleak. Actually, until I checked, I'd expected it to be shut. But open it was, and full of schoolchildren with clipboards and a photocopied project. Boisterous in their blue jerseys, not one of them (we believe and hope) bore the scars of a nightly parental flogging. But neither did they have young Johnnie's total enthusiasm for the natural world.

'This to me was a wonderful discovery,' Muir writes of a field mouse and her hairless pink young found in the foot of a corn stook. 'No hunter could

13

have been more excited on discovering a bear and her cubs in a wilderness den.'

'Ooh, that's minging!' exclaimed one small school-girl of today at their resin reproduction.

Mounted on orange card is a bedraggled feather, the remains of a genuine John Muir pen. The Birthplace Trust has yet to determine the species of its pen. For preference, Muir gathered his quills from the wild, and dipped if possible an eagle in his ink. That's when he was using ink. One impassioned letter to Mrs Professor Ezra Carr was written in sequoia sap.

A small glass screen is mounted on one wall, with a step below for small children. Here, says the sign, see the house where John lived from the age of three until he left Scotland. But instead of a video display, the screen is actually a small window, across the narrow alley, to the wind-scoured stone wall of the next-door house a metre away. (Austere Presbyterians make effective entrepreneurs, and Muir Senior expanded his premises and moved his family across.)

But the room's next corner has a genuine video screen, where I can sit aloof from the school kids and watch the great Yosemite waterfall, then see Half Dome, and the Merced River sparkling among its stones. And recall those trees almost as tall as wind turbines, that great bare granite. And here's a good resting place, the rucksack dumped in the reception area downstairs, Muir's pen a few feet away, the week's Muir quote on the wall reminding that: 'Cold writing is a feeble medium for heart-hot ideas.' The walls around me recapitulate the story I'd been told two months before, below those tall Sierra pines, on the trail to Tuolumne Meadow.

Notes and references

p7 (epigraph) John Muir: letter to Louie Muir from Dunbar, July 1893.

pp11–12 ('to gaze and wonder') John Muir: *The Story of My Boyhood and Youth*, Chapter 1.

p12 ('God's boundless mercy') Daniel Muir: letter, 19th March, 1874.

pp13–14 ('a wonderful discovery') John Muir: *The Story of My Boyhood and Youth*, Chapter 1.

2 The John Muir Way: Departing Dunbar

To-day I reached the sea. While I was yet many miles back in the palmy woods, I caught the scent of the salt sea breeze which, although I had so many years lived far from sea breezes, suddenly conjured up Dunbar, its rocky coast, winds and waves; and my whole childhood, that seemed to have utterly vanished in the New World, was now restored amid the Florida woods by that one breath from the sea. Forgotten were the palms and magnolias and the thousand flowers that enclosed me. I could see only dulse and tangle, long winged gulls, the Bass Rock in the Firth of Forth, and the old castle.

John Muir

Here's Muir in brief, as heard from a retired Yosemite ranger on the trail down from Cathedral Lake.

John Muir left Dunbar aged eleven for the harsh life of a pioneer farmer in Wisconsin. A life made even harsher by his father's prejudice against any form of activity other than seventeen-hour days of grindingly hard physical work (with a few hours off on Sundays). Even as a slightly undersized teenager, Muir was good at the grindingly hard work, earning the grudging respect of his father. John's toil enabled Daniel Muir to spend his own time in Bible study and zealous works of godliness and charity. In return he allowed his son as much time as he wanted for reading one or two books that weren't actually the Bible, and for experimentation in the workshop—just provided that time was before 5am when the workday began. Muir, accordingly, rose from his bed at one in the morning.

On leaving home he became an inventor and mechanic. For his own use he devised an alarmed bed with a mechanism that, when morning came, would tip him right out onto his feet. However, a file that he was using struck him in the eye, and for several weeks he was blind and in great pain. This event served, rather like his own internally-sprung bed, as an abrupt wake-up call.

Muir abandoned materialism, and at the age of 29 became a wanderer. He walked from the northern USA through to the Gulf of Mexico, 1,000 miles through a country still dangerous in the aftermath of the Civil War. His destination was South America, but there wasn't a boat, so he went to California instead. Landing at San Francisco, he enquired the

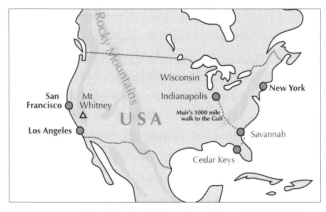

John Muir's 1,000-mile walk to the Gulf of Mexico

quickest way out of town to 'anywhere—just so long as it's wild'. The passers-by directed him to Yosemite.

After a spiritual Big Tree Experience in Yosemite, Muir explored the Sierras from end to end, named many of their mountains, revealed that those mountains had been landscaped by glaciers, and discovered the glacier remnants still lurking on the side of Mount Ritter. He grew a spectacular snowy beard and wrote eight slightly over-prosy books. Finally he persuaded the Americans to invent national parks and set them about with more protective regulations than anywhere I've ever been apart from the post-Communist countries of eastern Europe. (While actually walking the trail, I was tactful enough not to make this comparison of US park rules with those from behind the Iron Curtain—Americans, we know, carry guns…) He was the founding president of the Sierra Club, the USA's conservation pressure group. One year after his death, work started on the trail through the Sierra Nevada that bears his name.

Today's outdoor writers find Muir a handy source of sentimental landscape quotes: this has always put me off John Muir. His Trail is reputed the best long walk in the world. But is the man behind it actually any fun?

The business with the self-awakening bed gives a clue. Muir is indeed more than the prose Wordsworth of America. Up in the mountains he did things that were dangerous and uncomfortable. In his letters, and occasionally his more formal writings, he has a sense of the silly. His glacier studies are sharp-eyed but also passionate. And as a walker, he's way over the top.

In the end, Muir the man was to give me as many exciting moments and laughs, almost, as the long walk that bears his name. Walking the John Muir Trail, and after it the John Muir Way, would be an exploration not just of the Sierras and an odd corner of Scotland but of the concept of conservation and the ethics and aesthetics of outdoor fun.

But in Scotland, in 2007, winter sunlight was twinkling over the North Sea; and winter sunlight is short. Leaving the Muir Birthplace, I enquired for Davel Brae. This turns out to be, today, Victoria Street, and leads down to the harbour. Why Davel? The John Muir Trail is infested with black bears. But East Lothian's John Muir Way has something worse— body snatchers. William Burke of Edinburgh's West Port, hanged and anatomised in 1829, was very much alive in the night streets of Dunbar fifteen years later. In Davel Brae, Muir himself fled the

> *'Dandy Doctors,' clad in long black cloaks and supplied with a store of sticking-plaster of wondrous adhesiveness, [who] prowled at night about the country lanes and even the streets of the town, alert for unattended children. The Dandy Doctor's business method, as the servants explained it, was with lightning quickness to clap a sticking-plaster on the face of a scholar, covering mouth and nose, preventing breathing or crying for help, then pop us under his long black cloak and carry us to Edinburgh to be sold and sliced into small pieces for folk to learn how we were made.*

The story of Burke and Hare is well known, and not at all relevant to the life and walks of John Muir. But let's have it again anyway. The humane and practical 19th century saw transportation to the colonies replacing death as the penalty for most forms of petty crime. At the same time, after the Edinburgh Enlightenment of the previous fifty years, Edinburgh's Medical College was one of the most distinguished in the world. The result was a healthy black market in dead bodies for the university's marble dissecting tables. A fresh young corpse fetched up to £15— equivalent to several hundred pounds today.

When William Hare, keeper of a cheap lodging house in the West Port, had a lodger called Donald die on him, the handy way of recovering the man's back rent was to sell his one remaining asset—his corpse—to Dr Robert Knox of the medical school for £7, resulting in a handsome profit even after deducting the £4 back rent. The enterprising Hare then decided to streamline the production process. His next friendless and indigent lodger, Joseph the Miller, was plied with whisky and suffocated.

Others followed Donald and Joe to the dissecting tables: an unneeded distant relative of Burke's mistress, and one of the local prostitutes, who was unfortunately recognised by several of the students, her former clients, as they cut her up. Hare, with his accomplice William Burke, was responsible for sixteen or seventeen deaths and dissections in the twelve months their enterprise was running.

On their arrest, Hare turned King's evidence and escaped execution. Burke's hanging was one of the best-attended ever, with spectators queuing for six hours in darkness and pouring rain for a place around the gallows. At his own subsequent dissection there were unseemly scuffles, with stones and snowballs thrown at the police and 'several umbrellas were destroyed'. Hare suffered, at least in legend, an even worse fate. On his release from prison, he was seized by a mob and flung into a pit of lime, which blinded him and left him to spend the rest of his life as a street beggar. Their customer, Dr Knox, was not charged with any offence. And twenty years later, two older schoolboys were detailed to escort young Johnnie Muir up dark Davel Brae...

I left town past the derelict castle where Muir used to climb, and along a sea-ravaged sandstone coast where Muir played among rock pools whose small whirlpools, the sinister 'sookin-in-goats', were another threat to the town's youth. Perhaps it was surviving the Dandy Doctors and sookin-in-goats of

Dunbar that made Muir in later life so blasé about the rattlesnakes and bears of the Sierra Nevada.

Above East Linton, the tall blue signposts send me over a swell of yellow winter grassland—and there ahead was a way mark more striking even than the power station, the rocky cone of North Berwick Law. By dusk I was at its foot.

The John Muir Way skirts around this hill. But as a bit of miniature mountaineering it's not to be resisted. The last few metres I crawled into the wind, and fell into an rock hollow behind the trig point. There's a whale's jawbone mounted up here; it's been

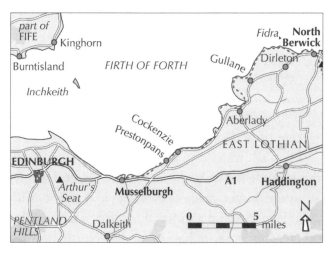

The John Muir Way (western half)

23

in place for 300 years, but in the darkness I didn't see it. What I did see was North Berwick, a sea of streetlights directly below. Across the dark firth, the Fife coast was a line of orange daisies along a midnight field. In the night and the wind I hung on to the trig pillar, and looked across the lights at the lump of darker darkness that was the Bass Rock.

A gale, on North Berwick Law, at December tea-time: this is by John Muir standards only mildly exciting. On the Yuba River in 1874 Muir passed a winter storm in a 100-foot spruce tree, swaying in a great arc across the darkness.

The slender tops fairly flapped and swished in the passionate torrent, bending and swirling backward and forward, round and round, tracing indescribable combinations of vertical and horizontal curves, while I clung with muscles firm braced, like a bobolink on a reed... One of the most beautiful and exhilarating storms I ever enjoyed in the Sierra.

Like all travellers, I eat wherever it's offered the local delicacy. At the end of the Muir Trail the Whitney Burger, made of buffaloes and cheese, with abundant fries and also the side salad. Thus, on this other Muir walk, it had to be the North Berwick Fry for haggis and chips, and the chip-shop dessert, fruit (tinned) under two scoops of ice cream topped off with generous squirts of cream from a canister. Served in a chunky cut-glass boat, this looked as good as it tasted, and like the Lone Pine diet under Mount Whitney, it is extremely healthy food, just provided you've been working hard all day under a rucksack or down a mine. My neighbour at the North Berwick Fry hadn't been. She overflowed the chair on both sides and made you wonder, or at least made my undisciplined imagination wonder, what she could possibly look like without her clothes on…

Small patches of wild country are not enough. Henry David Thoreau wanted the woods of Walden preserved as the huckleberry field for the inhabitants of Concord, Massachusetts. The landscape architect Frederick Law Olmsted retained Central Park as a rectangle of wild country within Manhattan's larger and exotically urban island. The John Muir Country Park, west of North Berwick, is a few square miles where wild birds can listen to the music of the motorway and contrast the moon with the orange glow of Edinburgh. The name itself is a giveaway: nobody would ever call Yosemite a 'Country' Park. East Lothian is basically a suburb with some surviving scrubby bits between the houses.

So what's this? At dawn on the third day, I emerged into a midget ecosystem every bit as interesting as the cloud forest of Tenerife or the glacier-scraped granite of the high Sierra. For two miles along the Lothian coastline the path wriggles through a sea-mangled shrubbery of thorny, bright-berried, buckthorn.

The branches are angular and bony and grey, twisted together from bush to bush; the berries cluster as thick as frogspawn, as orange as the streetlights of Edinburgh. A few oval, olive-coloured leaves dangle as autumn's afterthought among the berries. The ground below is a tangle of tough sticks, with stringy grass and the grey remains of plastic bags. The path is sandy and awkward, and the prickly branches snatch away the hat. Away on the right the sea grumbles beyond a beach of shingle, red basalt, and upended sandstone strata.

Muir found Edinburgh, when he visited it on his one return to Scotland at the age of 55, as 'far the most beautiful town I ever saw. I cannot conceive how it could be more beautiful.' Typically, his greatest approval was for the city's fine display of ice erosion: 'In the very heart of it rises the great Castle hill, glacier-sculpted and wild like a bit of Alaska.' Muir was probably aware that his ice-master hero, the geologist Louis Agassiz, had toured the city in

1840, and had disclosed the scouring of a glacier on Blackford Hill in the presence of the editor of *The Scotsman*.

But I found 21st-century Edinburgh clothed in bright pantomime garments: Christmas markets along Princes Street, helter-skelter and flashing fairy lights obscuring the dark basalt of Castle Rock. Porridge exotically flavoured with blueberries, white chocolate and sultanas: this is not a metaphor for Christmas Edinburgh but an actual stall, in the chilly shadow of the Scott Monument. Well, it's a metaphor as well.

Thinking about the place in today's exciting multi-ethnic world of honest porridge, I boarded my late-night bus for home.

Notes and references

p16 (epigraph) John Muir: *A Thousand Mile Walk to the Gulf,* Chapter 6. Journal written 23rd October, 1867.

p20 ('Dandy Doctors,') John Muir: *The Story of My Boyhood and Youth,* Chapter 1.

p22 ('several umbrellas') *The Scotsman,* 31st January, 1829, in the digital archive.

p24 (The slender tops') John Muir: *Mountains of California,* Chapter 10.

p27 Blueberry porridge, see www.stoatsporridgebars.co.uk

3 Yosemite to Half Dome

*Es ist dafür gesorgt, dass die Bäume nicht
in den Himmel wachsen.
(Care is taken over this: that the trees
should not grow into the sky.)*

Goethe

 In October 1849, as eleven year-old John Muir was preparing for his first, fierce winter in Wisconsin, two sawmill workers went hunting above the South Fork of the Merced River. The high pines are open enough for easy walking almost anywhere, but not open enough ever to see where you actually are. William Abrams and his friend were not accomplished hunters, and somewhere high in the foothills of the Sierra Nevada, they got lost.

Probably, they headed downhill looking for the green undergrowth that marks a stream. They noticed a bright place beyond the branches, and headed to it hoping for a view.

And a view is what they found. They emerged through a low stand of birch and manzanita scrub onto bare granite. That granite stopped abruptly in empty air. They looked down on tiny treetops, surrounded by great granite crags. On the left, that granite rose in a blank wall, 2,000 feet above their heads. On the right, a black angle in the rock face held a thread of white water, spreading to white smoke before it vanished behind the nearer treetops. (That's assuming the snows came late in '49. If there had already been snows to melt, the Bridal Veil would have been a wide thunder of falling waters.) And beyond and above the nearer cliffs, the great bare hump of Half Dome, its sliced face rising into the sky.

Yosemite from Inspiration Point

The tree mass across the valley floor was interrupted by the pale yellow of several clearings, where, if their eyes were sharp, they spotted Indian ponies grazing. Around those clearings, among the high pines, were shelters, several sweat lodges, a dance house, and acorn granaries—and a hundred or more of Ahwahneechee Indians, a subtribe of the Miwok, naming themselves from their refuge valley, 'Ahwahnee', the gaping mouth.

The Ahwahneechee were a quiet tribe, subsisting on creek trout, acorns, manzanita berries, and the game of the Sierra forests: bears, deer, elk, squirrels. Ahwahnee, long a spiritual sanctuary, had become a physical refuge as well, as the tribe had been increased by refugees, first from the Spanish, then from Mexicans slave-raiding for the plantations and farms of Sacramento. In that same year of 1849, American goldminers from the east reached the base of the Sierras, overgrazing the meadowlands, felling the oak groves whose acorns supplied the Indians' winter food, and burning down their villages. The Spanish with their missions had wanted the Ahwahneechee as Catholic converts; the Mexicans had wanted them as peons, slave labourers. The Americans just wanted them out of the way, or better, dead.

The dispossessed Indians had been raiding the

miners' camps for food. The State of California talked up this raiding into the 'Mariposa Indian War'. Is there some analogy here with today's 'War on Terror'? On 27th March, 1851, a 200-strong battalion entered Yosemite Valley. It burnt the villages, and pursued the Ahwahneechee up into Little Yosemite, but caught only one old woman.

Over the next four years, the Ahwahneechee were harassed out of the valley. By 1855, as the first tourists arrived at the foot of Half Dome, the Ahwahneechee were gone. And even their name for it had been lost. 'Yosemite' is usually given as *uzumati*, meaning grizzly bears in the Miwok language—and even the grizzly bear was to become extinct by the end of the century. But an alternate derivation has the invaders naming the valley after themselves. The Miwok named the white men of the Mariposa Battalion as *Yo-che-ma-te*: 'some of them are killers'.

Europe might have its ancient cathedrals, but California's outdoor ones were bigger and more ancient (and, incidentally, smelled of pine sap not papist incense).

The external appearance of this our dwelling place ... is fraught with lessons of high and holy meaning, only surpassed by the light of Revelation ... The Great Designer of these glorious pictures has placed them before us as types of the Divine attributes. (Asher Durand)

In the English Civil War 200 years earlier, Marvell and Milton had looked away from the battlefields to the green peace of England's forest remnants. In the same way, in its own Civil War, America could look to the high and holy trees of the Sierra, neither Union nor Confederate but far away in California. And so, in July 1864, Abraham Lincoln took a break from winning that war and went to Yosemite. He assigned Mariposa Grove and Yosemite Valley to the State of California as a protected state reserve. Along with an annual maintenance budget of $2,000—well, there was a war on. (In 1854, a working man earned about $1 a day, and a small town house cost $800. So this is about $500,000 in today's terms.)

Thirteen years after the first tourists, in 1868, John Muir arrived in Yosemite Valley. He lived there for the next eight years, working first as a shepherd, then in the sawmill (where his inventive skills improved the machinery) and as a part-time valley guide. Meanwhile he explored Yosemite and the surrounding Sierra, in summer and winter, with special attention to thunderstorms and blizzards.

The California state geologist had pronounced Half Dome as self-evidently unclimbable. It was, accordingly, climbed in 1875 by a resourceful black-smith using what would today be called artificial techniques. He set up his own *via ferrata* cable-assisted climbing route, which after various restorations is still used today. A few years later, Muir free-climbed it in winter conditions.

With a considerable impulse from two magazine articles by Muir, Yosemite National Park was founded in 1890, the second one in the world (after Yellowstone). By the 1950s, a million people were visiting each year. By the 1970s, it was two million. The National Park service set up traffic controls and a shuttle bus. In 2000, four million people visited Yosemite. In September 2007, Tom and I arrived.

We picked up our bear barrel, picked up our permit, and relaxed as we listened to the lecture about bears. If it goes on your outside or your insides, it goes in the bear barrel. Bears are experimental eaters. Suntan cream, haemorrhoid ointment…

Next morning we uploaded our big packs and made our first hesitant steps—right across the campsite to the big breakfast at Currie Village. All the all-American breakfast you can eat—waffles, bacon, hash browns, orange juice, biscuits and gravy, coffee, more coffee—for $10. That, at least, is the youth rate. If you're over 55, you only pay $8. This was the first benefit I have so far gained by my elderly status.

We wincingly shouldered our packs, and headed up the Mist Trail, which is steeper than the regular JMT but, as the name implies, lets you get sprayed by the waterfalls. The waterfalls were short of water (it had been a low-snow winter and a dry summer) but still were worth taking the steeper trails for.

Two hours up from the valley floor, we left the valley crowds behind us. Shafts of sunlight dappled the pine-needle path; the world smelt of pines, and hot dust. Above the treetops, the upper waterfall fell from somewhere that ought to have held nothing but blue sky. On the other side, bare granite just went on and on implausibly upwards. As the path zigged away from the river, we walked into the silence of the Sierras.

Up the trail, the water shortage continued. Rangers had said that the crucial Sunrise Creek was dry. This meant that we couldn't both ascend Half Dome tonight and also take the high route tomorrow over Clouds Rest: we wouldn't get enough to drink. 'But on the map there does seem to be, a bit further up, a stream beside the path?' I have suffered my first communication break-down—but then, I've only been in this foreign country for four days. After the ranger had looked blank for a bit, I worked it out: 'a *creek* beside the *trail…?*'

We ignored the ranger's water worries and went up Half Dome. The ascent of the cables and wide-spaced wooden steps is as exciting as it looks in the pictures. Late in the season, it wasn't too awkward passing the people coming down. Even so, the summit was a busy place. A couple of acres of flat stone, with a few mangled trees, and a whole lot of people wandering around looking over the edge in a bewildered sort of way. It was as if Trafalgar Square had been suddenly raised 5,000 feet vertically upwards into the sky.

The High Sierra, along with the rest of the Rockies, are part of the 'Ring of Fire' surrounding the Pacific Ocean. The cold, wet, heavy basalt of that ocean's bed is being dragged down underneath the American continent. Such 'subduction zones' are the primary cause of all the Earth's mountains. Any geology book will have, as its first diagram in Chapter One, a subduction zone.

Mountains above subduction zones are actively rising, and consequently are being actively worn down again by the weather. They are liable to earthquakes, and a bad one hit Lone Pine at the other end of the JMT in 1872. Continents grinding together underneath create friction heat, and subduction mountains are volcanic. Unusually, though, the hot rocks that bubbled up into the High Sierra do not take the form of lava and sky-fallen ash. Hot molten magma has risen here, but not right to the surface. Some miles underground it has cooled slowly, to make an underground lump of coarsely crystalline, pale-coloured, speckly granite.

That underground lump, as now revealed by erosion to form the High Sierra, stretches for 200 miles of glamorous granite. It is the biggest such lump in the world—Americans do tend to overdo things.

As the weight of the overlying ground is slowly carried away by rain, by rivers, and by ice, the granite expands. As it expands, it cracks. Layers of granite flake away, like the skin of a ripened onion. The effect is called 'exfoliation'; and who says geology doesn't affect our daily lives? Make your way up the steep side of Half Dome: the heat of the disappearing Pacific 100 miles below, the age-long melting of the bedrock, the erosion of several million years of glaciers, all these combine so that, as you reach the exfoliated layer edge, there's an awkward step up of several inches or even a couple of feet.

And the exfoliation steps are even more awkward on the way down…We've left our big packs all opened up, so that the varmints (chipmunks and squirrels) don't have to nibble holes in them on their way in. I'd wrapped my sleeping bag in two separate plastic bags. Leaving the outer one in place, the clever creatures have hauled the inner of the two out of the rucksack and nibbled some holes in that.

Half a mile on along the trail, we start exploring for a campsite near where the Sunrise Creek would be if it hadn't dried up.

'It's good, Dad!' shouts Thomas. Is he referring to the water trickle he's found or to the two good-looking young women who are busy filtering it? The young women head on down the trail; maybe we'll meet them again in the next 200 miles, but they do look quite quick. Our overnight neighbours are a family group who offer conversation about wildlife, and in particular, about bears. At Cathedral Lake the mother left the tent to enjoy the starlight—and saw two red eyes shining back at her torch. Thomas doesn't hear that bit and I don't pass it on: tomorrow night our planned camp is Cathedral Lake… They also offer an ingenious shower-bath, a water bag heated in the sun and hung in the trees with a sprinkler rose below. With only one day's sweat on our skins, we decline.

There would be hot water at Reds Meadow, only six days ahead.

As we had enough drinking water, we could divert off the JMT again to cross Clouds Rest. This gave us two hours of uphill, and so I guess some useful acclimatisation (Americans call it 'acclimation'). It also gave us great views back to Half Dome, and a little scrambling along the top. But soon we were back in the forest, looking at the tree trunks and wondering where our next water would be and whether there were any bears about. Plenty of trees, and some open meadows of yellow grass with granite crags above, led up to Cathedral Lake.

Notes and references

p28 (epigraph) Goethe: 'Wahrheit und Dichtung', epigraph, Part 3 (translation RT).

pp31–32 ('The external appearance') Asher Durand: 'Letters on Landscape Painting', in *The Crayon* 1855. Quoted in Simon Schama: *Landscape and Memory* (Vintage Books, 1996, and a five-part series on BBC television).

p32 English Civil War: see Marvell, 'The Garden', and Milton, 'Paradise Lost', Book IV, l. 139, a passage whose leaves rustle a century later within Coleridge's 'Kubla Khan'.

4 Cathedral Pass

I thought I should like to see his gait in running, so I made a sudden rush at him, shouting and swinging my hat… But to my dismay he did not run or show any sign of running. On the contrary, he stood his ground ready to fight and defend himself, lowered his head, thrust it forward, and looked sharply and fiercely at me. Then I suddenly began to fear that upon me would fall the work of running…

John Muir meets his first Sierra bear

Some days you eat the bear … and some days the bear eats you.

Stephen King

 Undoubtedly the most exciting way of getting dead in the great outdoors is the Black Bear. Bears are intelligent. Intelligent enough that when you hang your food on the small branch of a fir tree, they've worked out to send the bear cub to crawl out along the small branch and knock it down again.

In the 1960s, park rangers gave the bears pet names and fed them at car-parks. The bears became tame, and adept at breaking into cars. A touching sight, the ranger at Reds Meadow told me, the Mummy bear instructing the cub—put your claws around the top of the doorframe and just pull. To depart, do the same on the other side, thus avoiding broken glass. And so a car heads out of Yosemite, both front windows out sideways like a little aeroplane. Sweet!

The bear called Paradise Sue became skilful at scaring the humans away from the picnic tables, and had to be shot. Hence, today, if you hang your food in too short a tree, you don't just end up as a hungry hiker. You also get fined thousands of dollars for feeding junk food to the wildlife.

One ranger, when asked how bears can recognise even food hermetically sealed from the factory, said, 'Simple. They read the labels.' So how long will it take the intelligent bears to realise, we don't just carry food, we are food…? 'I knew that bears never eat men where berries and acorns abound,' Muir wrote in November 1871. What he means is, they haven't so far.

Of the stories we tell each other along the trail, at least half are bear stories. Of the jokes, almost all are bear jokes. How do you tell the difference between a black bear and a grizzly? Just climb a tree. If it's a black bear, it climbs up after you. If it's a grizzly, it pushes down the tree.

Bears, we know already, are adventurous eaters, and even lipsalve and medications have to be sealed away in the bear barrel. But one camper woke suddenly to find that a bear, seeking a new taste sensation, was licking the suntan lotion off his face… Each bear tale gets passed from northbound to southbound walkers, and spends all summer shuttling up and down the trail improving as it goes. The sun-cream story has got, as they say, strong legs. It has covered the entire Pacific Crest Trail in a couple of seasons, and is now heard in six separate mountain ranges.

In November 2007, it was reported that a bear had stolen a people carrier car in Vernon Township, New Jersey. The furry motorist released the handbrake, and rode for 50 feet before breaking out of the passenger side window and abandoning its vehicle. 'We knew it was a bear,' said Detective Sean Talt, 'because of the bear hairs all over the driver's seat.'

Scottish outdoor writer Chris Townsend, walking the whole Pacific Crest Trail, enjoyed a memorable bear encounter right here at Cathedral Lake. The bear passed through his own camp, ignoring the sealed bear barrel (the bears have learnt not to bother with canisters—just occasionally give one a swipe to make sure it's been properly closed). A few minutes later, amusing Chris if not those involved, the bear ran towards the forest with a food bag in its mouth, pursued by two naked campers.

John Muir lost his food cache to a bear in 1873. His punishment was a 40-mile walk to Yosemite and back for fresh supplies. Today he might have expected also a ticking-off from a park ranger, plus that stiff fine for improper food storage.

But we saw no bears, and the only naked people were in the far edge of Cathedral Lake, enjoying its shallow, sun-warmed waters. And above the bathers and Cathedral Lake, was Cathedral Peak…

We didn't find out if the swimmers were the women we'd seen earlier as they didn't have any clothes on and it might have been embarrassing. The lake was small by Scottish standards, but large enough for us to swim politely in the other edge. It was cool but not cold, a bit muddy across the bottom, a great place to float about and gaze at the granite summit overhead. The famous photographer of the Sierras Ansel Adams certainly missed a trick by not putting any naked women at the bottoms of the mountains in his pictures.

The women put their clothes on and strode away under their packs; but a photographer called Robert talked to us until he got so excited by the light that he had to start sticking his tripod into the shoreline.

Cathedral Peak

I was excited by the light myself, but embarrassed by my very small camera which didn't even have its exposure metre working. The real photographer kindly told me the light level and wanted to see what I'd got... Sorry, this camera's got slide-film in it, it's going to be weeks.

Robert the real photographer had two relations along to carry his 50lb of gear, but later was planning to rent a mule train and do it properly with 200lb of serious camera. A photographer earlier and even better than Ansel Adams, but whose name I've now forgotten, hiked the trails with two tons of gear, recording the 'Mountains of Light' (John Muir's nickname) on 36-inch glass plates. A creaking cart accompanied his every trek.

Actually, I wasn't completely thrilled by the light. Too clean and crisp, shadows too dark and rocks too pale: I missed the water-vapour tones of Scotland. Though I didn't miss the way that Scottish water vapour condenses and falls onto your head. Two full days of blue skies and dry feet. How long could this go on?

Our route plan suggested we might like to spend the next morning conquering Cathedral Peak (Class 3). Having looked at it all night, we didn't really want to.

If a certain Egyptian pyramid-builder had been in the habit of biting his toenails, or had an intimate companion to bite them for him, there would now be a path and large cairn on a fine high point of Wester Ross. Beinn Dearg is 2,998 feet—we only need to take 1/125 of an inch off the end of that ancient surveyor's foot to make Beinn Dearg into a Munro. And so, by some people's definition, a mountain.

Clearly the existence or otherwise of a mountain is far too important to be affected by the chiropody of antiquity. Indeed, it should be independent of the units used: 3,000 feet are no more significant than 1,728 megalithic yards or .000003 light seconds. Mountainousness must be inherent, and the discipline to determine it will be philosophy or nothing. Plato was a potholer—the Metaphor of the Cave indicates his choice of sport—but his theory applies to all sorts of outdoor activity and even to real life.

The so-called 'Real World' is a damp, dimly-lit cavern whose ferny entrance, could we but find it, leads out into the real Real World, the world of the Ideal. It's being born as human beings that has got us into this hole we're in. Yosemite is not limestone but granite, and so lacks caverns, but Plato's theory still applies. The Real World is the forest of sugar pines, where the hiker can only remember, and see in twiggy glimpses, the skies and blue mountains of the Ideal.

We recognise a mountain of here and now as being mountainous just because it resembles the half-remembered archetype, the Idea of Mountain. That Ideal Mountain can't be any other shape but that of the Matterhorn, as seen from Zermatt. Thus the Sierra Nevada has its own Matterhorn Peak, somewhere north of Yosemite. And Cathedral Peak, seen across its lake, is very close indeed to the correct mountain shape.

But is it the right height? For this, we need the altitude of that Matterhorn-shaped Ideal Mountain. Is it perhaps 4,572 metres, the height of the actual Matterhorn? But Mont Blanc is 4,642 metres. If the Ideal mountain height were 4,572 metres, then we would have to say that Mont Blanc would be more mountainous if it were 70 metres lower. This is nonsense. By the same token, Everest would only be improved by the addition of a proper summit, a Cathedral Peak affair overhanging the Kangshung Face, rather than the present arrangement of flat snow and oxygen cylinders.

Thus we conclude that the Ideal Mountain is at least 28,030 feet (8,849 metres). Every actual mountain of the real world is, it transpires, too low.

And the Platonic Ideal of the Bagging List is not the Scottish Munros, or the 14,000-ers of the USA, but an empty page.

Notes and references

p39 (epigraph) John Muir: *My First Summer in the Sierra.*

p39 (epigraph) Stephen King: *The Girl Who Loved Tom Gordon* (Scribner, 1999) (King's ellipsis).

p40 ('bears never eat men') John Muir, quoted in W F Badè: *The Life and Letters of John Muir,* Chapter IX.

p45 Chiropody of antiquity. Or by addition of a prosthetic summit, such as the one made of fibreglass carried onto Beinn Dearg by *Trail* magazine in the 1990s. Foinaven, in Sutherland, is similarly 914 metres and 2,998 feet high. Both are, by any sensibly subjective criterion, more mountainous than the Munro-height Beinn Deargs of Atholl and Loch Broom.

5 Lyell Canyon and Garnet Lake

Hiking—I don't like either the word or the thing. People ought to saunter in the mountains—not hike! Do you know the origin of that word 'saunter?' It's a beautiful word. Away back in the Middle Ages people used to go on pilgrimages to the Holy Land, and when people in the villages through which they passed asked where they were going, they would reply, 'A la sainte terre,' 'To the Holy Land.' ... Now these mountains are our Holy Land, and we ought to saunter through them reverently, not 'hike' through them.

John Muir

Another overnight neighbour accompanied us the next morning, improving some dull forest with interesting information. Some of the information was about John Muir, about whom we were then so woefully ill informed, and was summarised in Chapter 2. The rest of it, of course, was about bears. And there are a lot of trees for them to be hiding behind, down 3,000 feet of zigzag trail to Tuolumne Meadow.

Here we heard car engines among the tree trunks, though the JMT doesn't actually cross any tarmac in its 210 miles. We enjoyed a Tuolumne breakfast. It consisted of biscuits and gravy, grits, shredded bacon, waffles and coffee. Biscuits and gravy, grits, shredded bacon, waffles and coffee weren't quite enough, so we had breakfast again. Then we did some shopping.

Having enjoyed Cathedral Lake so much, we headed up to an even higher lake for the third night out (unnamed on our map, below Donohue Pass). Here I discovered the one culinary subtlety of the boiling-water-into-the-bag freeze-dried cuisine. It's formulated for 5,000 feet. At 10,000 feet, water boils cooler. Obey the packet, leave it for ten mins before eating, and you get some meaty treat that's indigestibly undercooked. The trick is to reseal, wrap in a fleece jacket, and leave for one and a half times as long. *Bon appetit!*

Only a handful of daily permits are handed out for the Muir Trail. In September, we were meeting just one or two other expeditions each day. But each night, there would be somewhere around the lakeside interesting Americans to talk to after the undercooked heat'n'eat. As Americans go, though, these trail types are not typical. Well, we know the average American walks 400 metres a day. But also, 30 per cent of

Americans voted for G W Bush; and every single one of the trail types apologised about that fact.

The Americans on this third night knew all about Scotland as they had ancestors from there. More: 'Oh yes, we went to Scotland. We were in, what's your city called...? Dublin.'

Using, we hope, sounder geography, they were planning ascents of Mount Lyell, the highest in Yosemite National Park. We took it easier. Having reached the bleak stony Donohue Pass, we dumped the rucksacks and set off up the bleak stony Donohue Peak. The guidebook (by R J Secor) had promised Class 2 scrambling, but it was a walk with some entertaining boulder-clambering to finish. The 1,000 feet of ascent above the pass took us to 12,000 feet and left us breathless. But while the pass below gave bleak crag-hung views, the summit gave views of a different sort: distant spiky summits and quite a lot of lakes. Such leaving of the well-prepared smooth trail, and of the heavy rucksacks, for a few hours of wilder country and wider views: this is a way of making the 'World's best walk' even better.

Granite all the way could get a little dull. Only so many times can you exclaim over exciting large feldspar crystals (pale pink rectangles, the size of match boxes, scattered through the grey granite). But given that the granite forms a huge, once-underground lump, if you keep walking uphill through it, you eventually come out among whatever the granite lump melted its way up into. This happens for the first time at Island Pass. Above the pale granite slopes rise mountains that are black. And by the time we reach Thousand Island Lake, we've walked up off the granite into something quite different.

These overlying black rocks are clearly volcanic. Instead of the big sweep of granite, the rocks are

Donohue Pass

blobby; here and there they show bubble holes where gases have emerged from the hot lava.

But a minute later the underfoot rock field, while still black, is slaty. Some of the slates are striped with green. Severe compression sideways is what makes slates. And when what's being compressed is black basalt, and if it gets really well squeezed, the result is green jade. Well, strictly, jade is the gemstone: the mineral it's a pure form of is jadeite. Or else it's another mineral indistinguishable from jadeite called nephrite.

Geology, like computer studies, has picked up world-wide words and put them in its pockets. Aa lava from Hawaii flows onto greywacke from Germany and gets hollowed into arêtes from the French Alps and corries from Scotland. Below Mammoth Crest, we would tread on pebbles in metamorphic rocks that have got rolled out into squashy cylinders: that is *boudinisation*, from a sort of Belgian sausage. This makes you feel, with your nose in a geology tome, like some sort of world poet.

Except here at Thousand Island Lake. The rock that has green jadeite as its main mineral is called 'jadeitite'.

But geology needn't be poetic so long as it's practical. If we only had a geological map, we could determine how far we'd have to walk to get off these sharp slates and camp back on comfortable gravelly granite.

This fourth day ended alongside Garnet Lake, still on the black slaty stuff, but at a campsite of overpowering loveliness. A family party invited us to share their dining area. As usual, they had ancestors from Scotland.

'And just remind me,' asked the son-in-law: 'What's the name of the channel of water that divides Scotland from England?' We have to tell that, despite the best efforts of the Scottish Assembly, there still isn't one.

Bill, the patriarch of the party, has a taste for Spam. Not junk emails, but the ground-up meat in a tin that got Britain through World War Two. And it must be good trail food, for when the varmints got into his bear barrel they ignored the peanut butter and the freeze-dried packets, but ate up all of his Spam. And what's the British English word for 'varmints'? We don't have any? How ever do we manage…?

The big Bill party was slightly embarrassed that its day's saunter had been a mere three miles from Thousand Island Lake, so close indeed as to have the identical view of Mounts Ritter and Banner. Tom and I were embarrassed at having hiked a coarse and excessive fifteen miles. We didn't even mention being up Donohue Peak; it just would have made us dreary athletes without the proper attitude.

The slower you go, the more you need to carry. And the more you carry, the slower you have to go. But this does work also in reverse. You can leave behind a whole lot of food, walk a bit more briskly, and find that the food that you didn't bring, you don't actually now need.

Guidebooks at this point say: but of course, such haste defeats the whole purpose of the Trail. Walking hard and head-down, you ignore the beauties of the landscape, you miss out on the wildlife, all for the trivial pleasure of making the rest of us feel like pathetic slowcoaches.

But this isn't a guidebook, so I don't have to say that. And besides, I really do try to be polite and broadminded and not claim any special merit in less-slow travel—fifteen miles a day with 3,000 feet of ascent isn't actually *fast*, there are people on the trail doing twice as much. And maybe we are missing out on the nuances of the landscape, not spotting that red-tailed hawk, but if we see less intensely we see more in miles.

That's what I say when I'm being polite. It's not true. Kevin Saunders, a Yellowstone guide, spent several days sitting six feet off the trail with a clipboard; six feet off the trail but in plain sight. None of the trail users saw him. Saunders was worrying over the average distance at which a hiker first becomes aware of a bear, which is around fourteen feet. He puts it down to poles: a poled walker is peering at the trail, not the scenery. Poles, yes; but I also put it down to packs. With 50lb on your back, the upper body bends forward, and even on the JMT's easy paths, each pole placement is a crucial support. It wouldn't do to stumble and end up upside down in a patch of poison ivy. And the bear, when she does leap out from fourteen feet away and tear your legs off, probably comes as a blessed relief from the blisters…

We writers have a duty to the sensitivities, but also to truth and the English language. If you take all day to walk ten miles, then a pathetic slowcoach is exactly what you are. Muir's disparagement of hikers came from his later years ('during an early Sierra Club outing'—so after 1892, when he was about 60). He could hike 40 miles a day if fancy or necessity impelled, and his 1,000-mile walk to the Gulf, of 1867, averaged twenty miles a day.

However, all this campfire talk, of speediness and of Spam, was distracted by the tall cone of Banner Peak, slowly going black against the sky.

Notes and references

p48 (epigraph) John Muir: conversation recorded by Albert Palmer in *The Mountain Trail and Its Message* (Boston, The Pilgrim Press, 1911; and Sierra Club website). The origin of 'hike' is obscure. Muir's derivation of 'saunter' is out of an essay, 'On Walking', by H D Thoreau. Slightly less fancifully, 'saunter' may be from French, *s'aventurer*, to go out adventuring as a knight errant. Which comes to much the same!

6 Devil's Postpile

Beautiful blueberries

Chris McCandless

 At 6am, the first light crept into the open end of our tarp tent. The tall cone of Banner Peak stood grey, now, above a silvery lake. Then, as the daylight strengthened, the mountain turned miraculously pink. The external glow warmed our hearts, though it did little for our frozen fingers. We wondered whether to wake up the neighbours, so they too could freeze their fingers and look at the pinkness of Banner Peak and its higher neighbour, Mount Ritter.

In October 1884, John Muir approached Mount Ritter through the canyon country to its north. After a bivvy without blanket, by a small lake at 11,000 feet, he set off just before sunrise with a crust tied to his belt. With light snow cover and some verglas on the rocks, it was too late in the season to attempt the mountain's first ascent—but he would head up the base of it anyway, just to have a look. He mounted a slope of hard snow above Lake Catherine to reach the

Ritter/Banner col. He continued into a steep couloir (nowadays a snow-free chute) 'just for the view'. Soon he had climbed ground too serious for him to want to reverse it. The 'just having a look' trick is still used today by climbers needing to deceive themselves they're not actually setting off on a climb.

He was now committed to the couloir, with 1,000 feet of unknown ground above him. Even supposing he got to the summit, he had no idea how he might get down again. The couloir ran up to a steep rock wall. The easy ways up the couloir sides proved smooth and holdless, and at this point his usual confidence began to desert him:

Therefore, after scanning its face again and again, I began to scale [the couloir headwall], picking my holds with intense caution. After gaining a point about halfway to the top, I was suddenly brought to a dead stop, with arms outspread, clinging close to the face of the rock, unable to move hand or foot either up or down. My doom appeared fixed. I must fall. There would be a moment of bewilderment, and then a lifeless rumble down the one general precipice to the glacier below.

When this final danger flashed upon me, I became nerve-shaken for the first time since setting foot on the mountains, and my mind seemed to fill

Mount Ritter (left) and Banner Peak from Garnet Lake

with a stifling smoke. But this terrible eclipse lasted only a moment, when life blazed forth again with preternatural clearness… My trembling muscles became firm again, every rift and flaw in the rock was seen as through a microscope, and my limbs moved with a positiveness and precision with which I seemed to have nothing at all to do. Had I been borne aloft upon wings, my deliverance could not have been more complete.

The adrenaline surge, familiar to any mountaineer who's got into a dodgy situation, carries him on through broken rock towers and spurs to the sunlit summit. There he pauses. He observes the difference between the glacier-smoothed surroundings and the peaks that formerly stood above the ice as nunatak islands. No time for geology! What about getting down? Casting about, he discovers the reasonably easy route by the south-east glacier, whose only disadvantage—apart from the short ice-fall (now another stony chute) near the bottom—is a walk of several hours, into the beginning of the night, to return around the mountain, and also Banner Peak, to rejoin his food and his jacket.

Back at his camp, he lies 'loose and lost' for a while in that pleasant state as the body scours its blood system for spare atoms of energy so as to embark on the evening chores. He lights a 'sunrise fire'—a particularly big and orange one—and enjoys a simple supper of dry bread, cold water and hot tea. His North Face ascent route—without snow-cover, black ice, and some of its 19th-century glacier—is now graded at Class 3, a serious scramble.

Trees and lakes led down to Reds Meadow, and the Devil's Postpile. It's impressive, even if not quite at the standard of Staffa in Scotland (but then, I haven't been to Staffa yet). A lunchtime arrival let us, luckily, reach the cafe early enough for supper—it has to be booked by 3pm and eaten at precisely 5.45. It also left time for a short hike through burnt-out pines to Rainbow Falls. They were only just worth the effort, as they left just fifteen minutes for Reds Meadow's unique facility.

In Japan it would be *onsen*, the natural hot pool set around with stone benches, alongside a pristine pre-wash zone and fluffy towels. At Reds it's a concrete shower block. But the shower needs no fiddling with the settings, and never goes cold, and perhaps the Japanese do go to a whole lot of unnecessary bother. After all, there are plenty of tasteful aesthetic effects outside among the mountains.

Reds' shop is running itself down ready for the winter snows. There is a poor choice of vegetarian freeze-dried delicacies. There is no, not none, zilch-oh, peanut butter. No peanut butter! Have we perhaps strayed into an enclave of Europe? (No. There is also zilch-oh in muesli and in marmite.) What they do have is a JMT visitors' book. The two women ahead are Primrose and Chanson, and they sign themselves with peace signs and little flowers. Sadly, however, once we've sorted out the American way of writing dates inside out, they are 24 hours ahead. Still, there are just enough people to talk to up and down the trail, and no nasty ones so far. 'That's one thing about being on the JMT. It's like being in a small town that's three feet wide and two hundred and eleven mile long.'

We reach the Mulehouse Café, damp-haired and only a couple of minutes late, and thus get seventeen minutes for the devouring of a big, green salad. I feel the vitamins insinuating themselves into my fingertips and battered toe ends. Then comes the pork chop or the vegetarian option. And would we like the blueberry pie? And given that we would, would we like it 'à la mode'?

For the first time since I incautiously attended a lecture on English Literature at Cambridge University, I was unable to understand the English language at all. I do understand French, and *à la mode* is 'in the style'—which doesn't help. It actually means, 'with ice-cream'. We want it with ice-cream.

What we didn't realise was quite how much we wanted, alongside the ice-cream, the blueberries. Yes, they are a new wonder food containing antioxidants, whatever those may be. But they also feed into the deep myth of the American wilderness. The myth of the Huckleberry, and Henry David Thoreau.

'Go a-granging among oranges and bananas and all such blazing red-hot fruit,' writes Muir. 'For me, I like better the huckleberries of the cool glacial bogs.'

But first, we need to distinguish between the blueberry and the huckleberry. Which can't, actually, be done. A huckleberry belongs to one of three species of genus *Gaylussacia*, conceptually separated off from *Vaccinium* in 1898. A blueberry belongs to the remaining sixteen species of *Vaccinium*. Alternatively, a blueberry is a blue berry that, when you cut it, is white inside. A huckleberry is blue all through. These two definitions overlap, but do not coincide. What's a blueberry in one state, or in one wood, is a huckleberry in another. Or else it's a bleuet, or a sparkleberry.

The Scottish bilberry or blaeberry (*Vaccinium myrtillus*) has also been known as a hurtleberry (perhaps from its bruised purple colour) or whortleberry. 'Huckleberry' is derived from hurtleberry. But whatever a huckleberry may be, it ain't a bilberry.

Henry David Thoreau starts one of his essays by explaining that the things that matter most of all are the unimportant ones, such as huckleberries. Accordingly, he is going to discuss, over 33 pages, the huckleberry. He discusses the six different species of huckleberry, and sneers at any idea that Britain with its bilberries has claim to huckleberry hegemony. He speculates for a couple of pages on the supposed huckleberries of classical antiquity, such as may have decorated Mounts Ida and Olympus. He reserves special commendation for the hairy huckleberry, the one species of the seven that is not just nasty but actually inedible.

In those days before computer games, paperback books, and long-distance walking trails, they took their amusements where they found them. The Huckleberry essay originated as a public lecture—a lecture of 33,000 words lasting, by my calculation, an hour and a half. After all, none of the audience is hurrying home to catch the baseball.

Half an hour into the huckleberries, HDT touches on the ecology of small shrubs, and discusses their importance in the diet of the Algonquin Indians. That said, they were also important to the Iroquois; and to the Narragansett. And the Abenaki. Oh, and also the Sioux. Actually, while we're on the subject, both the Delawares and the Chippeway Indians were also enthusiastic consumers. By this time the audience is realising it would have been more exciting to sit at home staring at the wall while waiting for the invention of television…

Next comes a tip for youthful huckleberry gatherers. Use your mother's coffee pot. The huckleberries you eat on the way home can be made up by holding down the lid and giving the pot a gentle shake. Then there's the useful lesson in practical jurisprudence, as each gatherer claims his section of the hill.

But alas, that in the degenerate 1850s there is already opening a gulf between the gatherers of the huckleberries and those who eat the resulting pie. Huckleberry hills are fenced, and taken into ownership; huckleberries are sold for cold cash in the market. 'It is as if the hangman were to perform the marriage ceremony.' And widening his scope, even wild country that happens to lack huckleberries may still be worthy of preservation. 'I think that each town should have a park, or rather a primitive forest... where a stick should never be cut for fuel—nor for the navy, nor to make wagons, but stand and decay for higher uses—a common possession forever.' And he suggests in particular that Walden Wood—Walden, where he lived—'might have been reserved... might have been our huckleberry field.'

The bean-field and the huckleberry patch: the civilised East and the wilderness of the West; or, in Mark Twain's classic pair of novels, Tom Sawyer and Huckleberry Finn. Is it coincidence that Twain's wild boy shares his name with Thoreau's plant essay of fifteen years earlier? We have to imagine Twain in the Hartford Connecticut public library: 'What, no Hemingway yet? No Elmore Leonard? Guess I'll have to haul out that heavy-looking Henry David Thoreau…'

Huck Finn himself was banned from the public library in Concord, Massachusetts—Henry David's own home branch. The purging person was Louisa May Alcott, lady authoress of the nauseating classic *Little Women*. But she missed the more subtly subversive *Studies in the Sierra*, published two years earlier by a certain John Muir.

Seventy-five years later, in the film *Breakfast at Tiffany's*, party girl Holly Golightly sits on the outside staircase with a guitar and metaphorically contrasts New York City with Moon River, and a small berry-bearing shrub, 'my huckleberry friend'. Having Audrey Hepburn sing it (which her character doesn't do in the original novel by Truman Capote) has to be credited to director Blake Edwards. Great song lyrics don't need to explain themselves. The 'huckleberry friend' is the river itself between its trees; or a sharer of her childhood berry bucket; or, obliquely, Huckleberry Finn himself.

Today Walden Pond lies under the traffic noise of major roads on either side; the ground where HDT lived in chaste communion with his bean-field is overrun with early-morning joggers. It has indeed, as he suggested, been preserved, complete with car park, gravel walkway, and a reproduction hut. But Thoreau's words, in his 1851 essay on Walking, that 'in Wildness is the preservation of the World', were picked up fifty years later by John Muir.

Thousands of tired, nerve-shaken, overcivilized people are beginning to find out that going to the mountains is going home; that wilderness is a necessity; and that mountain parks and reservations are useful not only as fountains of timber and irrigating rivers, but fountains of life.

Notes and references

p57 (epigraph) Chris McCandless: final journal entry before starving to death, Alaska, August 1992. Quoted in Jon Krakauer, *Into the Wild* (Villard/Random House, 1996).

pp58–59 John Muir: *The Mountains of California*, Chapter 4.

p62 ('That's one thing about being on the JMT') 'Pyro' Jim Robertson, internet journal, August 1996.

pp62–63 ('Go a-granging') John Muir: letter to Mrs Ezra Carr, December 1874.

p63 H D Thoreau essay: 'Huckleberries'. In *Collected Essays and Poems* (The Library of America, 2001).

p66 'Moon River', 1961. Johnny Mercer/Henry Mancini.

p67 John Muir: *Our National Parks,* 1901.

7 Mammoth Crest

Nel mezzo del cammin di nostra vita
mi ritrovai per una selva oscura
ché la diritta via era smarrita.

(Midway along the pathway of my life
I found myself within a darkened wood
Where the straight trail was lost from me and gone.)

Dante

 It's about ten million years since humans came down out of the trees. Straight away we headed out into open country, where the sun shone on our newly-bald bodies, where we could see the hills, and walk up them without getting poked in the eye by a twig.

Authentic oakwood is grim. Nettles and brambles attack your ankles, while between the tree trunks wolves, bears and brigands leap out and kill you. Real ancient woodland is rotten wood tangled together with honeysuckle. It's great for beetles and tree creepers; not bad if you're a Native American lying in wait to ambush the noisy and incompetent paleface. But not nice if you're a walker going for a walk.

Jaques, in Shakespeare's *As You Like It*, heads into the Forest of Arden specifically to enjoy his own miserableness. Dante's great poem exploring the realms of Hell and Paradise starts off with him wandering into a darksome wood and getting off the path. The forest is where, if you lose your trail of breadcrumbs, you'll end up in the witch's oven as a tasty Sunday roast. As the TV historian Simon Schama has written:

> *From Ireland to Bohemia, penitents fled from the temptations of the world into the woodland depths. In solitude, they would deliver themselves to mystic transports, or prevail over the demonic powers lurking in the darkness… a site of miracles, where stags would appear bearing the Holy Cross in their antlers.*

In odd corners of England, the Green Man with his beheading axe dwells among the holly and the ivy below some ancient semi-natural oaks. In Poland or Ukraine, it's a wood of spruce that the witch Baba Yaga tempts you into with trippy agaric toadstools. And wild spruce woods, such as grow below the Julian Alps of Slovenia, are indeed uniquely gloomy.

Even on New York's Broadway, *Into the Woods* is where you 'have to make the journey', whether you're a prince, a poor boy needing to trade in your scrofulous cow, or Little Red Riding Hood bringing back Grandma's shopping. The bent fairytale has music and lyrics by Stephen Sondheim.

It took me a while to get the point. At Yosemite—Yosemite of the giant redwoods, cult site for John Muir and for sixteen couples performing the cotillion without the least discomfort on the sawn-off pine trunk—I was mostly peering between the trees to see if I could see the mountains. Descending from Clouds Rest, I was glad of the shade but, after four or five hours, happier to emerge to a grassy meadow and some lumps of granite overhead.

But on our fifth day we'd decided on another high-level diversion, over the Mammoth Crest. And this was an interesting one, involving sections of wild pathlessness. A mile of compass work through a pine forest: it's just orienteering, like we do in the woods at home. But somehow it's more serious when, if we get it wrong, the forest goes on, and on, for several days of walking.

At this point I ought to quote J Fenimore Cooper. But for me, the writer who holds the soul of America somewhere among the twisted innards of his Apple Mac is—look the other way, please, you serious literary types—the horror writer Stephen King. Well, sales figures anywhere under 100,000 are not fully

American, and who buys Fenimore Cooper? And the sea of trees that starts behind the final suburban picket fence and goes on effectively for ever—inhabited by ancient spirits, bears of course, and also (but not in Fenimore C) deranged humans in orange hunting jackets—where are they but in Stephen King? Nine year-old Trisha heads down a side trail for a pee, short-cuts back across the junction—and fails to find the main path. Bramble-scratched, bleeding and hungry, she beds down under a pine branch, and tunes in on her Sony Walkman to the Boston Red Sox baseball team. Will the personal radio be enough to save her from whatever is tearing resin-bleeding holes in the pine trunks and leaving disembowelled forest creatures across her path? This is Stephen King, where small things are big: so perhaps closing striker Tom Gordon, whispered into the headphones, will indeed do the trick.

But in the High Sierras, there are no radio stations to bring comfort in the darkness under the big trees. 'When I would recreate myself,' writes Henry David Thoreau, 'I seek the darkest wood... There is the strength.' Obviously he's never chased after a bear in a state of serious undress.

Even a small cloud in the relentlessly blue sky counts

as a weather sign. One fluffy white one at 11am becomes several by noon, overcast an hour later, and a thunderstorm late in the afternoon. And well before eleven, that fluffy white cloud was bouncing about in the sky. All the same, a mile on a compass-bearing through some trees: this is serious in Stephen King but not in the real Sierra. Shortly we're up on a thinly wooded ridge. Well-made zigzags (in US-speak, switchbacks) lead quickly up 3,000 feet, which is just as well, as by the time we're on the ridge the noon clouds have thickened up. But we'll be along and off before the afternoon storm.

The views are hazy. This doesn't matter, as the ridgeline under our feet is amazing. After six days of almost entirely granite, where the most exciting formation was that clump of feldspar crystals (actually, I find the feldspar pretty exciting, but then I am writing a book about rocks and stuff just now) … anyway, here is volcanic rubble, red crusty clinker from a coal fire that burnt too hot. The black boulders have holes in like Emmental cheese, which is where the gases boiled out. And all this only 10,000 years ago, which in geological terms is as recent as our last lunch-stop.

On the left, black crags drop to dirty snowfields a long, long way below. But then—several hours before thunderstorm time, though it doesn't really look as if there's going to be one—the trail drops off into a cragged hollow with two small lakes. There the trail comes to an end. Perhaps there may be a way out through the gap at the back, but the map makes it forbiddingly steep. The other possible route has some more of that dirty snow…

This could all get exciting. But spoiling the suspense, a walker comes towards us, a walker who has just passed into the cragged hollow by way of the forbiddingly steep gap, which he tells us is going to have a small path. Never mind. That small path leads

Duck Lake

out to Duck Lake, where for two miles we romp down a well-made trail across a steep slope with the lake at the bottom and an extremely shapely mountain rising on the other side. Thunder rumbles, and lightning may well be striking that extremely shapely mountain. And so we continue to Purple Lake. Every American has fifteen minutes of fame, and every American walk has twenty minutes of rain. This one does, anyway; and they take place at Purple Lake.

Notes and references

p68 (epigraph) Dante: *Inferno*, opening canto (translation RT).

p69 Simon Schama: *Landscape & Memory*, (Vintage Books, 1996).

p71 Stephen King: *The Girl Who Loved Tom Gordon* (Scribner, 1999).

p71 ('darkest wood') H D Thoreau: 'On Walking'.

8 Pocket Meadow

There are so many lakes in these hills and so few geographers that they began to run out of ideas. Tonight is Purple Lake, in a zone where they're named after colours. (Sorry, 'colors'.) Last night was Reds Meadow, the night before was at Garnet Lake in jewel-name country. Tomorrow night will be at Vermilion. Reds, Garnet, Purple, Vermilion. Neat, or what?

First lake of the new day is Virginia, in a zone of girls' names. Later in the walk, Lakes Wanda and Helen on either side of the Muir Pass are named after John Muir's daughters. Every guide to the JMT feels obliged to mention this, and then to list the altitude of every one of the eleven or so passes, even if the whole 210 miles are compressed into just 800 words as they are in the *Trekking Atlas of the World*. I thought in this present book I'd get my Muir Daughters mention out of the way early. His wife was called Louie: there is no Lake Louie.

Anyway, on no evidence at all, I'm surmising that the girly lakes are named for each of the women he ever slept with. How else could you come to name a lake Evelyn or Hortense? There is also, of course, Lake

George, not to mention Lake of the Lone Indian. But JM was an adventurous sort of fellow…

Silver Pass is the one of the eleven that when I look back I can't recall at all. And being short of film, I haven't even a photo of it. But Tom reminds me it was where I was wanting, in the arid dust and stone-fields, a lone human skeleton to complete the scene. Shucks, no skeleton—that'll be why I didn't bother with the photo. Below the pass, the trail drops off excitingly into a granite hollow and then a whole

John Muir: self portrait

lot of trees. Rangers with spades stopped work to make pleasant conversation: 'How's it going, guys?' We knew, because we'd been told by walkers coming towards us, that this was the hypocritical softening up before a demand for our permit. And so it proved. They were out 'iceberging'. Rangers disapprove of various possible camp sites, such as those within 100 feet of lakes, streams or the trail, or those on living grassland. These park employees were planting large projecting boulders—icebergs—in the middle of any such site. We didn't enquire whether they were doing their camp-site sabotage as volunteers, or if they were getting paid.

The last mile under the trees was hot and long. But Edison Lake had shrunk, due to a dry summer and also dam repair works. This gave us another last hot mile across the dry lake bed to the speedboat that replaced the ferry. At the edge of the dried mud, we flopped like stranded fish for half an hour until the boat came.

People from outside the UK laugh at the Lake District for being a national park without any wolves. But the Lake District ceased to be wilderness about the time they set up the stone-axe factory on Harrison Stickle. The swamp dwellers of Langdale complained about the noise and the scar on the scenery from all the loose chippings—before getting hold of the cool new axes, shafting them with their toughest bits of stick, and proceeding to clear the native tree cover. Three thousand years later, the National Park authority was installed, not to preserve long-vanished trees, but to prevent the Forestry Commission from planting even more.

Given that the Lake District park people manage to annoy both rambling man and Mr Business, they must have made a reasonable fist of the developers vs nature impossibility. But abroad is another historical era. They'll do things differently then. Switzerland has a rather different notion of a National Park; there, money always takes priority over the mountain. A few years ago, the Swiss decided to equip with chains the Zmutt Ridge of the Matterhorn—thus converting a fine mountaineering route into an easy way for guided parties. This was done to relieve pressure on the two ridges already in chains, and increase by 50 per cent the income derived from the mountain. If we followed the Swiss example, there would be red-and-white paint flashes up Striding Edge and a cable car to the top of Ben Lomond. Loch Avon would have a mountain hotel, with helicopter landings. There would be an iron ladder up Broad Stand; fixed ropes or a carved-out path to ease the passage along Sharp Edge; and, of course, a funicular railway up Cairn Gorm.

The Carpathians take up where the Alps leave off—a 4,000-mile crumple-zone from the Vienna Woods to the Black Sea via Ukraine, Hungary, and Romania. The Tatras, half in Poland and half in Slovakia, are their pride and highpoint. Among the world's big mountain ranges, the Tatras are the smallest. It's a wonderland of granite spires that's—er—twice the height of the Lake District (up to 2,655 metres) but only half as wide.

This hill group has the arduous duty of being the main range in Poland. And there are a lot more walking Poles in Poland than walking poles in Lochaber and the Lake District added together. And of course, walking Poles do damage the environment. In addition to being Poland's main range, the Tatras are the main range of Slovakia—and the Slovaks are no slouches. At the same time, the Tatras are a proper National Park: they have wolves, and bears, and a few unhappy eagles flapping around looking for a flat bit without a picnicking Pole.

The Tatras, whether Polish or Slovakian, are ex-Communist hills. Some of the ex-Communist commissars have ended up in the National Park. In

Poland they wear a red jumper, in Slovakia they wear a green fleece and a badge, and they do like to keep you under control. You may not walk after an hour before sunset, or before an hour after sunrise. You may not cycle or camp. You may not hang-glide—it bothers the eagle. (The Polish Tatras, like England, have just one eagle.) The paths are marked with stripy signs in red, green, yellow, blue and black, and on the paths is where you walk. Those paths are, on the whole, stone-cobbled ones. Rugged stairways of granite wind up through the dwarf pine scrub into bouldery corries, twiddle around among some lochans, and zigzag fearsomely up a slope of stones to a tiny pass between two granite spires. The last few metres to the col are a simple scramble assisted with a fixed chain, and through the gap you see a new stony corrie, some more lochans, and some more granite spires.

Mountains are born free, but everywhere in Europe we see them in chains. And no, I don't want an iron ladder up Skye's Inaccessible Pinnacle, though there is that awkward pitch above the top of the Bhasteir Tooth, it is a bit out of place when the rest of that bit of ridge is so easy… But Poland's not my country, and I don't have to heartsearch about the morality of it all. I just have to heartsearch about the iron ladder with 1,000 feet of empty air instead of a bottom rung.

A bit of Stalinist legacy can allow certain short-cuts. (No, not the short-cuts between the zigzags of the waymarked path—there's the man in the red jumper and an on-the-spot fine for those.) They don't ask the climbing club if it would like to stop parking its motor cars in the mudbath at the top of the Chocholowska valley, and they don't ask the Chocholowskans about the drop in ice-cream revenue. They just close the road. And then they re-open it to a troop of horse-drawn taxis that are as slow as walking but a whole lot more expensive.

Straight away, the valley smells of dung rather than diesel and the hills have got a bit bigger. And just imagine this applied to Scotland. Park and ride all the way along the Highland Line, with a return of the steamer service up the West Coast from Glasgow. Lochnagar a two-day walk in from Kirriemuir, or maybe take it from the train at Blair Atholl—why, that makes Lochnagar as big as the Matterhorn.

And as you walk past the Polish pole barrier at the bottom of the closed road, what's this but a rustically shingled, log-sided, ethnic traditional tollbooth. They make you pay for the park! What you pay is 3 Zloty, the equivalent of 40p in our money. But never mind that, it's a fundamental principle of democracy that footpath damage should be paid for out of general taxation. It costs to go to the opera and that's quite right because opera is for toffs. But the parks are for the people and the people don't pay. It's in the Arbroath Declaration of King Robert the Bruce.

It wouldn't work in Scotland because they wouldn't charge us 40p, they'd charge us £25. And once they started excluding, they'd exclude us from all Knoydart for the sake of the sea eagle. In Scotland, so far, there just isn't the people pressure. When the man with the people-counter won't let you up Giewont (the Sleeping Knight), it's because Giewont's top is about twice the size of the top of Sgurr nan Gillean, and last week someone at one end sneezed and someone at the other end fell over the edge.

Wild Places for Nature and People—this is a slogan at the moment of the John Muir Trust. This is like the washing-up liquid that's tough on grease but kind to your hands. It's like the energy bar that's nourishing but not fattening. If you want people and nature, then both people and nature are going to take a bit of punishment. (But speaking personally, you can hang me in chains from Poland's Orla Perc any time.)

If you want the freedom of the wilderness, it seems, you gotta have some wilderness regulations. Behind the sometime Iron Curtain, you may not camp at night: you could, in principle, be excluded for failing in your duty of cheerfully greeting your fellow walkers. In the Land of the Free, you must camp 100 feet from the trail, you mustn't cut short the switchbacks, you must do your doo-doos in a little plastic bag.

Polish people are closer to their rural origins. You won't find an unpicked bilberry beside any Polish mountain path. And down in the woods you wouldn't want to look, as every side-path is lined with piles of Polish poo. Is the Pope Polish? Do Poles shit in the woods? He was, and his favourite Tatra hut was the one called Morskie Oko. They do, and they leave the same gay pink and blue paper streamers as we see spreading like prayer flags over the high ground in the English national parks. But we are a free people: and a free people doesn't poo into any plastic bag.

Notes and references

p75 Trekking Atlas of the World (New Holland, 2008) with, incidentally, some pictures of Tom in various European hotspots, but whose pictures of the JMT persuaded my mother-in-law that she might be about to lose one of her favourite grandsons.

p76 John Muir self portrait: drawing in letter to Miss Janet Douglass Moores, 23rd February, 1887.

9 Vermilion Resort

Vermilion is one of the world's great walker stop-offs: we might think of the Jermoso Hut in Spain's Picos de Europa, or Ossian Youth Hostel in the middle of Rannoch Moor. We might think about the monks on the Great St Bernard Pass, who invented the concept of hospitality. Vermilion has a useful shop, but also a bear-proof barrel at the entrance where you can pick over other walkers' abandoned food before deploying your own credit card. Vermilion has all you can eat for about $10, and all you can eat is a lot. There are veggie options for vegetarians like Tom, and high-grease options for high-greasians like me. There are pre-erected bunk-bed tents, looking left over from the Korean War, which you can sleep in if there's space.

'You can come in with us, hi, I'm Primrose.'

In which case, that has to be Chanson.

'I think we saw you already… at Cathedral Lake?'

'Did you take a photograph?'

'I told him not to,' says Thomas apologetically. But they really were a long way away. And any mountain scene, even Cathedral Peak, is improved by some naked women in it...

Campfires glow late into the night—well, 8pm is late night for us. The stars are bright in this clean air so far from any streetlight. In their honour, an impressively bearded solo walker called Dan sings us the whole of the Monty Python Galaxy song. Some cannabis adds its aroma to the pine smoke rising from the brazier. The two young women have been resting up for a day, at minimal expense.

'This boy bought me three beers and told me I was a free spirit,' says Primrose with a slightly bewildered air. Even Thomas, at age 25 here cast as a worldly-wise older male, smiles at that one. Conversation ranges across the Universe, then suddenly homes in on the exact ounces in various sorts of sleeping mat.

And here, if nowhere else in the West, the oral tradition of story-telling still survives. There's the trail tale about the suntan cream; and even the joke about black bears and grizzlies, gathered by me off one of last year's JMT walkers, seems fresh here.

And then there's Nine-Eleven: what really happened. It's known that a 747 isn't heavy enough to penetrate a building. Dust that spread across Manhattan afterwards was the residue not of burning fuel but of high explosive. The two aircraft, robotically controlled, fired cruise missiles to break into the buildings. It was all engineered by the Bush administration to provide an excuse for the Iraq invasion.

Amazingly, the administration managed to deceive all the world's major newspapers, and the many TV cameramen, but not the French conspiracy theorist Thierry Meyssan, whose book *L'Effroyable Imposture* is in English as *The Big Lie*. Meyssan's theory actually suggested that the impact on the Pentagon (not the Twin Towers) was caused by a missile rather than an aeroplane. With American Airlines red and blue stripes painted on the sides to mislead all the eyewitnesses whose evidence might otherwise have interfered with the theory. Meyssan's book sold 20,000 copies in two hours in France.

Primrose, pre-trail, had been at the Burning Man Festival (which involves standing around in a sandstorm with no clothes on). The Korean war tent-hut is her first bed for several weeks, and the mattress is so exciting she has trouble getting to sleep.

'Chanson, that boy who paid for our meal tonight, what was his name can you remember…?'

With the extra mud section, it turned out to be no shorter taking the ferry back to the trail than heading direct, up the Bear Ridge Trail. An approaching walker eight days back had suggested the Bear Ridge: a walker five days back had said it was unpleasant and dusty. But it did mean not having to wait until nine o'clock for the boat trip. So we did it. And everybody else followed us, so that I felt guilty for depriving the ferryman of his morning revenue. The trail was a less-used one, and off the edge of the map, so for the second (and in fact final) time we used our compass and some navigation.

'Funny thing,' impressively bearded Dan had slipped into the bear conversation, 'but whenever I'm on a geographical feature named for a bear, a bear is what I see.'

I tapped my walking poles on every tree trunk, I wanted to make sure that the bear was going to see me and wasn't too worried if I didn't see the bear.

After a day of Bear Ridge and Bear Creek, mostly under branches but happily bearless, we emerged to Marie Lake. 'Marie, wow, amazing in bed' as it doesn't say in John Muir's *My First Summer in the Sierra;* but it was in truth an amazing night with the evening light caressing several ranges of pointy summits to the north-east.

At dusk a hiker in black with a big rucksack came along the shoreline and pitched alongside. It was Jim from Georgia, whom we'd met several times due to his habit of walking rather slowly under his heavy backpack (as I should have referred to the rucksack in the previous sentence) intersecting with our habit of going off sideways to visit nearby peaks.

The Georgian accent is particularly pleasant, or, perhaps, Georgians are just pleasant people. John Muir liked them a lot, as he walked to the Gulf of Mexico in the aftermath of the American Civil War.

> Of the people of the States that I have now passed, I best like the Georgians. They have charming manners, and their dwellings are mostly larger and better than those of adjacent States. However costly or ornamental their homes or their manners, they do not, like those of the New Englander, appear as the fruits of intense and painful sacrifice and training, but are entirely divested of artificial weights and measures, and seem to pervade and twine about their characters as spontaneous growths with the durability and charm of living nature.
>
> In particular, Georgians, even the commonest, have a most charmingly cordial way of saying to strangers, as they proceed on their journey, 'I wish you well, sir.'

Jim from Georgia is comfortably self-sufficient —but not from choice. He's waiting for his grandchildren to get older so they can come along. Jim, who lives quite close to it, is the only person we met who actually likes the other long walk, the Appalachian Trail. Even so, a main pleasure was the many interesting towns you could get to by leaving the trail by a short bus trip. Tom's girlfriend's home is in close to the Appalachian Trail but I don't think I'll be walking it even so.

More company was around the lakeside in the shapes of some fishing rods, some beer, and three men in their forties—a combination that we met in several friendly incarnations along the way.

Next morning's side trip was Mount Senger. The guidebook makes it a simple walk. It isn't a simple walk: it's a lot better than that. What looks from below like a ridgeline turns out to be a pile of jammed boulders. Clamber onto a rock the size of half a house, then wander along its top to climb the next half-house boulder. At the top it steepens, and has drops below, and the climbing is less light-hearted. The holds up here have been weathered by 60 feet of snow every winter. The rock is washing-machine clean, but its projecting quartz crystals would do horrible things to any merely mechanical washing machine.

Alongside the ridge, miles of blue air lead to the next ridge of the jagged granite. Between the peaks, in a wide bowl of stones, small lakes are scattered like paint splashes from when they coloured in the sky. Beyond and below that, a darker hollow is the place where we're seeing dirt, and trees, and all that messy stuff called organic life.

At the very top, the ridgeline steepened again and finished through a small hole. British scramble grade 2, I'd say, good big holds but quite steep and exposed (ie, with a drop below). Anywhere in the UK, it would be a crowded classic, with people picnicking on every ledge. As it was, the summit notebook made us the first people up Mount Senger for three days.

We descended an easier way, on slopes of crystal sand and scree. In the boulderfield at the bottom were the remains of someone's pack frame, and a sleeping bag laid across a rock with a stone on top. Inside the sleeping bag there was, however, no skeleton. The remnants were well faded: we guessed that someone had left their gear on the way up, been caught in snow or thunderstorm, and made it out down the other side of the mountain.

Having had our scrambling fun, we headed down through more trees to Muir Trail Ranch.

Mount Senger summit

Muir Trail Ranch is not like Vermilion. At Muir Trail, they're more interested in horses than in hikers. For 46 dollars each they'd hauled in two plastic buckets full of food and stored them for us in their varmint-proof shed. It took two hours to pack it all into the bear barrels, find it wouldn't fit, decide what to leave behind, and then pack it all in again. My friend Jeff had assured me that seven days' food would fit into one bear barrel. But he'd also revealed that he'd lost 12lb in weight on the trail. Tom hasn't got 12lb of weight to spare, and I'm not much better fleshed myself.

As we arrived, Jim from Georgia was unpacking his own food bucket. Soon he was commencing to put on his reloaded rucksack. Ten minutes later, after crouching beneath, knees gradually straightened, groans, twitches, and shoulder shrugs, the rucksack was finally in place. From Muir Trail Ranch to the end, there's nowhere to take on food. It all has to be carried: seven days' worth of it. Or, if you're reading the guidebook and taking it easy along the trail, eleven days. For months I'd been wondering about the seven days of food. How many days would we walk before it started being fun again? Would we walk at all? We evaded the issue by putting some of the food back into the varmint-proof shed for the night and heading out to the hot spring.

The sophistication of the Japanese-style hot spring experience was, once again, not there. The pool was separated from the surrounding meadow by a half-rotten pine log. It was muddy at the edges and gravel in the middle. Some romantic soul had stuck a few candle-ends to the rotted log. We thought it was just great. We were soggy and wrinkled right through, and the stars were starting to show, by the time we splashed back through the San Joaquin River to our camp.

Notes and references

p86 Thierry Meyssan: *9/11 The Big Lie* (Carnot, 2002).

p86 ('2,000 copies in two hours') *Rough Guide to Conspiracy Theories,* 2005.

p88 John Muir: *A Thousand Mile Walk to the Gulf.* Journal written Autumn 1867.

10 Evolution Basin

'Try not the pass' may sound in our ears, but despite the solemn warning ... the passes will be tried until the end of time, in the face of every danger or rock, avalanche and blinding storm. And whatever the immediate motive may be that starts us on our travels—wild landscapes, or adventures, or mere love of gain, the passes themselves will in the end be found better than anything to which they directly lead.

John Muir

 In Scotland you walk up a mountain, move on to another mountain, and then walk back to the car. In the Sierra Nevada, it takes a day and more to cross a single pass.

We start our climbing of the Muir Pass at Piute trail junction on the San Joaquin River. The altitude is 8,000 feet. The Muir Pass is out of sight and will remain so for the whole of the day ahead. In fact, as we are underneath some very high pine trees, everything there is, is out of sight, except for a patch of sky. The path scarcely seems uphill but it must be, as after two hours the pines are smaller and less dense.

Between their tops we see a broad, U-shaped canyon whose upper slopes are slabs of granite. The granite is decorated with ledges, and layers of pines. But where an avalanche has swept down some time in the last century, the granite is quite bare.

Between the pine trunks is the gleam of the river. The path emerges to sunshine beside the water, and we look upstream to where blocky rock towers peer into the top of the glen. No gap leads through between them; in fact they are mere spurs, and our way will lead through somewhere else. A wooden footbridge crosses the river, its handrails hot under the sun, its underside lit by flickers off the water. Two hundred paces further on, the path turns abruptly up the canyon side.

It takes ten minutes to adjust the pace and the breathing, to make unwilling legs learn the new angle. Granite slabs appear, white gleams among the tree trunks. The path zigzags a dozen times. The trees up here are even smaller: the sun comes between, heating the forest floor and releasing the summery pine resin smells. Instead of looking up through tree trunks at crags, we are now looking across at one of the upper mountains, the tall tower of the Hermit (which at 12,300 feet is about the height that our eventual pass will be). The river has changed its nature. It pours down granite slabs in splashy white, lingers in a green pool, and slides away down the next of the slabs. Despite the heat of the mid-morning, where the water sprays onto an overhanging branch an icicle has formed.

Two zigzags up, a park volunteer is working with bucket and hammer. The path-building season is now in its final week; they've been up here for three months. We can understand why he's looking forward to a wash.

'Oh,' he says, 'I bathe every morning. There's always a lake or a creek.'

'But didn't you see the ice back there?'

'Yes, that's why I'm looking forward to hot water.'

Our legs have got used to it; and we're surprised how soon the path levels. Bits of broken tree let us cross the stream without freezing our toes off. This upper valley is a classic hanging one: smooth-floored and U-sided, but smaller than the San Joaquin. And the extra altitude means that the trees give way to open yellow meadows. The stream spreads wide, golden boulders emerging from deep blue waters that reflect the big sky overhead. The afternoon saunters by. We dip our toes in the cold creek, we eat crackers and peanut butter, we sterilise some water. We meet the ranger and report the abandoned equipment on

Mount Senger, three days walk down the trail. As we're eating the peanut butter we are passed by the heavily burdened Jim from Georgia.

And now the trail rises again, bare slabs among the trees. Then it's bare slabs in the open, slabs scoured by the giant Brillo-pad of the glacier, and into a closed-in world of rock, gravel, and wide blue water. Around the Evolution Lake twisted trees stand, just enough to break the bleakness. Ahead and on both sides, rock rises to jagged ridges. Despite the sun, the air is cold; and the lake water is clear and clean. Jim from Georgia has already dropped his big black pack, but out of friendliness decides to follow us up to an even higher lake, where we'll be better placed for tomorrow's pass.

As we walk into the evening the shadows stretch across the lake, the trees thin out, the ground gets bleaker. It also gets lumpier. There are no flat places beside the path, so we head down across rocks towards the head of the upper lake. In the shadows among the boulders, two tents are already in position. We find a wide gravel ledge, sheltered by crags above, and put the tent up. Our neighbours are reading *Far from the Madding Crowd* in the last of the sunlight, but twenty feet below them we are already in the shades of evening. We unpack briskly, put on all our spare clothing, and do not linger over our food. Georgia Jim does not appear. I imagine him somewhere in the rocks, legs in the air, trapped by his pack like an inverted beetle. We did not, in fact, meet Jim again. (But two days later, overtaking walkers did report his tent in a meadow a few hours behind us.)

At dawn, golden sunlight crept down the crag slopes: golden light that had no warmth in it whatever. We walked up into thin and stringy grasses that didn't hold even a memory of greenness. This was the last outpost of biology. Above was bare rock, and slopes of stones—and the lake behind us was rightly called Sapphire, as its blue seemed of the mineral kingdom. We had passed above all growing things, and were also at the top edge of the granite. The crags above the lake were black basalt: and the line of it ran across the granite slopes as blatant as spilt ink on a clean white page.

This lake, so bleak and bare—together with its twin beyond the Muir pass—these are the two that Muir chose to name for his two daughters Helen and Wanda. Did Muir subscribe to the idea that highest is nicest, irrespective? Alternatively, did he dislike his daughters? No to both. For Muir, these two blue jewels in their setting of untrammelled geology were, simply, the best lakes of them all.

The boulderslope tilts, steeply enough that the path resorts to more zigzags. Ice leans against the surrounding slopes: ice that's as dirty and old as snow-piles in a city street. The air is thin, so that even a gentle zigzag is an effort. But with life already gone, things can't actually get any bleaker. Always, there's one more zigzag. But eventually, a long hard hour above the lake, there isn't. Among the stones is a shelter, built like a stone-roofed monkish cell. Behind it, the ground drops to Helen, the other sapphire sterile lake; and far beyond and below, a haze of green trees. We have reached the top of the pass.

Josiah Whitney, geologist to the state of California, has already got one thing quite wrong in this book —back in Chapter 3, it was him asserting that Half Dome would never get an ascent. He misunderstood the valley underneath it as well. The towering rock walls of Yosemite, the sharply defined valley floor: these, clearly, were not the effect of normal mountain wear and tear. These were some cataclysm, a collapse of the entire earth's crust.

Does Whitney really deserve to have the end-point of the trail, and the high point of the contiguous USA, named after him? He does. He does anyway, for being on the Yosemite Commission that persuaded

President Lincoln to cede the valley to the State of California as a state reserve, at a time when the young Muir was away in Canada dodging the American Civil War. But he does, too, for his wrong science. Wrong science is good science when it's clearly stated and lucid enough to be disproved. Whitney derided Muir as an 'ignoramus' and a 'mere sheepherder'. Whitney's survey reports suppressed evidence of glaciers. Without Whitney's wrong geology, not to mention the insulting epithets, would Muir have looked so hard at the talus piles below El Capitan, the scarred slopes of Half Dome, and the hundred valleys of the hinterland? Have seen and studied, over several years, so as to demonstrate convincingly the wrongness of Mr Whitney?

Well, yes, he probably would. He arrived already with his head full of that modern man Louis Agassiz and his Ice Theory. And Muir, whatever we may speculate about his sex life, was as a geologist both randy and passionate.

I found out a noble truth concerning the Merced moraines that escaped me hitherto. Civilisation and fever and all the morbidness that has been hooted at me have not dimmed my glacial eye, and I care to live only to entice people to look at Nature's loveliness.

The upper end of the main Sacramento valley is covered with ancient river drift and I wandered over many square miles of it. In every pebble I could hear the sounds of running water. The whole deposit is a poem whose many books and chapters form the geological Vedas of our glorious state.

But glaciers, dear friend—ice is only another form of terrestrial love.

The drift and the moraines are piles of rubble dumped by the now absent glaciers. Across the upper valley floors, and half-way up their sides, the rocks are smoothed by the glacier. And the stone you stand on is grooved and scratched in the direction of that glacier's flow.

But this is nonsense, as the early critics of Agassiz pointed out. Ice is slippery, not rough. And while it is hard, it is still softer than the rocks that it has supposedly been scratching. However, glaciers have crevasses—cracks that sometimes run right down to the bottom of the ice. Stones and boulders fall in, and are dragged along by the moving ice. The glacier is, in effect, a sheet of extremely coarse sandpaper. In the UK, glacier scratches are underneath the moss and lichen, or have been washed by 20,000 years of rain. In the Sierra, there isn't any moss and lichen; and the rocks lie under snow for nine months of the year and under sunshine the rest. So the scratches—striations, or *striae* for those who like their vowels well jammed up—are clear and everywhere. In one place, below the Palisades Lakes, the rock had a set of C-shaped scratches nestling together in a band: rather like the gathers in the rufflette tape where you put the curtain hooks into your curtains. The C-scratches are chatter marks, where a boulder has been dragged like fingernails on a blackboard, but much—much—slower and more agonising.

At the top of the valley, on the slopes of Mount Goddard and Black Giant, are the dying remains of the glaciers themselves. No gleaming ice, but dirty grey under their rubble and, sadly, not going to be there at all for much longer. It was Muir who, having identified the ice action in the Yosemite valley, went on to discover the remnants of still-living ice on the mountains above. Mount Whitney itself retains two small ice fields. Whitney himself, however, died in heroic ignorance in 1896, still denying that there are current glaciers in the Sierra Nevada.

Notes and references

p94 (epigraph) John Muir: *Picturesque California*, Chapter 2.

pp100–101 ('a noble truth') John Muir: from letters to Mrs Ezra Carr, October 1874, May 1875 and December 1871.

11 Le Conte Canyon

Our vegetable love shall grow
Vaster than empires, and more slow

Marvell

 The readers of *Far from the Madding Crowd* had three things to tell us:

• What the national park people issue dreadful warnings against is a hypothetical, not an actual, danger. The water in the Sierras has fewer harmful bacteria than the San Francisco public supply—and San Francisco is particularly proud of its water supply.

• If we like peaks alongside the path, Black Giant is a straightforward, but scenic, walk-up.

• A hurricane is approaching, and will arrive on Thursday week. It will drop several feet of snow. Hikers will have to be extracted by helicopter.

These propositions gave us something to discuss as we hauled our overweight packs up the zigzags of Muir Pass. The passes so far had been at around 11,000 feet. Muir Pass represented an abrupt jump up, being the first of the 12,000-footers. When, from its summit, we looked at Black Giant, we decided not to believe the overnight neighbours about its being a walk-up. For consistency, we decided not to believe them about the hurricane coming as well.

The disadvantage of this was continuing with the hassle of sterilising the drinking water.

We decided instead to climb Mount Solomons, as a break from the big rucksacks. Theodore S Solomons was the obnoxious little lad of 14 who, born in the 1870s and thus deprived of such healthy pleasures as computer gaming and alcopops, hit on the idea of a high-level Sierra trail. Mount

Mount Solomons scramble

Solomons rises to 13,000 feet proudly above the high point of that eventual trail. Mount Solomons, as it happens, is a heap of rubble. As we climbed we wondered whether it was going to come down and join us quicker than we could get up on it. But the view from the top repaid all. Directly in the west, Charybdis, Scylla, and the Three Sirens are rock obstacles from the wanderings of Ulysses, whose own Homeric hike was undertaken in a boat. The Black Giant looked even blacker from up here, and roughly twice as gigantic. The junction line of the pale granite with the older black volcanic on top: this showed especially well on Mount Goddard, next one around from Black Giant. Far away in the northwest, Mounts Banner and Ritter looked very small, as they certainly should do after seven long days of walking away from them.

Descending from Muir Pass is a wonderful mix-up of pale granite and black basalt. 'I hope you won't be publishing any of these boring geology photos you're taking,' says Tom.

The path went on and on downwards, past small lakes, over granite slabs, into Le Conte Canyon, named after the geologist who was the first to believe John Muir about the Sierra Nevada glaciers. More huge granite dangled overhead—or perhaps it was black basalt. We couldn't tell, as we walked for hours hidden under the sugar pines, the Douglas firs, and the aspens. For on the Muir Trail, as in Life itself, after every excursion to the sunlight and the granite summits comes a descent into the green gloom.

Five million years ago, humanity clambered down out of the trees, stood up on its hind legs, and strode out into the wide, sunlit savannah. Why go back now?

Well, some people really go for the green gloom. *Throughout all this glorious region, there is nothing that so constantly interests and challenges the admiration of the traveller as the belts of forest through which he passes.*

In 1852 a hunter called Augustus T Dowd went out after bear steaks, but discovered some sequoias.

'Come and see the big grizzly I found,' he joked to the gold miners. The miners, forty-niners still there with shattered illusions three years later, probably didn't laugh a lot at finding 250 feet of timber instead of their supper. But the big trees of the Calaveras Grove, in the foothills below Yosemite Valley, got nicknamed as the 'Grizzlies'. Thus forming a random correspondence with the Miwok *uzumati*, grizzly bears, that (for those who don't believe the derivation I gave in Chapter 3) gave their name to Yosemite itself.

The biggest tree of all, 90 feet round its base, had its bark stripped and shipped east, then reassembled in New York. The sophisticated New Yorkers refused to believe in the bark; meanwhile the tree itself died. So they chopped it down, and on 4th July, 1855, 32 persons were engaged in dancing cotillion on the exposed stump, without any of them falling off the edge.

The giant redwood was named as *Wellingtonia* by UK botanists. Fortunately, French biologists decided that it was related to the coast redwood, which was already named as *Sequoia sempervirens*. 'Sequoia', the name of the Native American who compiled the written form of Cherokee, is arbitrary but at least is not a British military commander. Instead, individual big trees would be named after military commanders of America.

The discoverers of the sequoia groves were amazed not simply by their size but by their biblical age: these trees were already full grown while Solomon was calling in the builders of his temple to discuss their cost overruns. In fact the world's oldest trees are bristlecone pines found in White Mountains, just across Owens Valley from the Sierra Nevada. But those are scrawny, damaged things quite lacking in splendour.

Whether the sequoias are also the world's biggest living things has also been questioned by pedants. It depends what you mean by 'thing'. In the year 2000, a giant honey fungus *Armillaria ostoyae* was found killing trees over 2,200 acres (three and a half square miles) in the Blue Mountains of Oregon. The toadstool crosses three county lines and is almost as old as a giant redwood. But it might merely be an assemblage of genetically identical brown and smelly individuals. Scrubby aspens, *Populus tremuloides*, which supply a splash of bright autumn yellow in the deep green gloom, are, technically, bigger individuals than the redwoods towering overhead. Cheekily, the aspens are single-genome colonies with connected root systems, and one, the Pando 'grove' in Utah, covers nearly 100 acres and weighs 6,600 tons. This is roughly the three biggest sequoias added together. And then there's a four-mile piece of seaweed, *Posidonia oceanica*, discovered floating around Mallorca.

But no seaweed or scrubby aspen can rival the giant redwoods. And let's not even think about any smelly fungus. The three biggest living things on the face of the planet are as follows:

		height (feet)	circumference (feet)	volume (cubic feet)
1	General Sherman Giant Forest, Sequoia NP	275	103	52,500
2	Washington Giant Forest, Sequoia NP	255	101	47,850
3	General Grant Grant Grove, Kings Canyon	268	107.5	46,600

William T Sherman was the most brutal of the Union commanders in the Civil War (and became a tank in World War Two). He burned Atlanta and deliberately caused $100 million of property damage on his 'March to the Sea'. In the song 'Marching Through Georgia', those sweet potatoes were not leaping from the ground of their own accord. In this sense Sherman can be called a creator of wilderness, if in a different way from John Muir, who passed through devastated Georgia on his own walk to the sea three years later.

General Grant, on the other hand, was the second most brutal of the Union commanders. As a tree, he rivalled Sherman to the point of almost reigniting civil war between Kings Canyon and Sequoia. For in this context, what counts as big? For mountains, height is all. But slender coast redwoods reach 368 feet in height without being counted as the biggest. The American Forestry Association's points system put neither of the two brutal generals as the top tree. So they fudged the points system to let Sherman win.

Both are ugly things, splitting half way up into massive chunky branches each bigger than any tree east of the Mississippi. Their tops have been repeatedly burnt out by lightning strikes. Sherman is perhaps the uglier, and in 1965 President Lyndon Johnson nominated General Grant as 'the nation's Christmas tree'. Grant, as US president, founded the first National Park (Yellowstone, as it happens, not Yosemite). He also was the one who made Xmas a federal holiday. (LBJ was probably not aware of that, though.)

Another of the big trees is named for President Andrew Jackson. This is particularly appropriate as Jackson the man was nicknamed after a tree, 'Old Hickory'. And given their status as a symbol of national reconciliation, it's only appropriate that two should be named for Confederate General Robert E Lee. National reconciliation only goes so far. The Lee trees are two of the smaller big trees: the one in Kings Canyon National Park is barely 22 feet in diameter and 254 feet high.

The Enlightenment of the 18th century took an axe to God. Man, as a reasoning being, was to stand self-erect in the sunlit clearing among the stumps that had formerly cast the green gloom of organised religion. The centre isn't us, but the Sun. Man didn't arise from dust at God's command but descended, for no reason at all, out of apes. The world was created not in the six days so splendidly orchestrated by Haydn in 1798, but over millions of years.

The Romantics, and in this context the Lakes poets Wordsworth and Coleridge, raised the feelings of man, alongside his reasoning intelligence, to stand in the sunlit clearing. Their projects were landscape appreciation, communal lifestyles, drugs, poetry, and fell-walking.

American poet Walt Whitman takes the Romantic project even further. He elevates the feelings not alongside, but above, the critical and creative intelligence. His poems were, accordingly, obnoxious to right-thinking Americans. The New England Society for the Suppression of Vice, in 1882, persuaded his publisher to withdraw *Leaves of Grass*:

It is I, you women, I make my way,
I am stern, acrid, large, undissuadable, but I
love you,
I do not hurt you any more than is necessary for
you,
I pour the stuff to start sons and daughters fit for
these States,
I press with slow rude muscle

Censorship is evil, and also un-American. Even so, the Suppressors of Vice do have a point here—though the one about Californian redwoods which I shall quote below was not found unacceptably sensual and overt. It would be left to John Muir to explore the sexuality of the sequoia...

Have I suggested that Americans tend, occasionally, to overdo things? The overdone, American, version of the English Lakes poets is known as Transcendentalism. Whitman's verse followed a poetic programme laid out by Ralph Waldo Emerson. The other prophet of Transcendentalism was Henry David Thoreau. *Walden* is about self-sufficiency. Thoreau persuades himself—and after himself, in slow and measured prose, the World—that the good life is under the branches of the wild wood, looking after a field of beans. The hoe is the way to go.

Muir, an enthusiastic reader of both of them, could have found himself foreshadowed in their works.

I lay down the book and go to my well for water, and lo! there I meet the servant of the Brahmin, priest of Brahma, and Vishnu and Indra, who still sits in his temple on the Ganges reading the Vedas, or dwells at the root of a tree with his crust and water-jug. (Thoreau)

We have had many harbingers and forerunners; but of a purely spiritual life, history has afforded no example. I mean, we have yet no man who has leaned entirely on his character, and eaten angels' food; who, trusting to his sentiments, found life made of miracles; who, working for universal aims, found himself fed, he knew not how; clothed, sheltered, and weaponed, he knew not how, and yet it was done by his own hands. (Emerson)

Much to Muir's excitement, in 1871 Ralph Waldo Emerson visited Yosemite. Muir left a letter at Emerson's lodging, and the two met up the following day.

I invite you join me in a month's worship with Nature in the high temples of the great Sierra Crown beyond our holy Yosemite. It will cost you nothing save the time & very little of that for you will be mostly in Eternity.

But Emerson, already 68 years old, was persuaded by the rest of his party to be sensible in a nice warm bed rather than sensual under the sequoias.

Pantheism is the belief that the natural world is a direct manifestation of the divine. Nature is God, and God is the natural world. Yosemite's sequoias are better cathedrals than most cathedrals; the vision from Half Dome at sunrise is a spiritual vision; and—for a seriously passionate pantheist—plants, stones and boulders are alive, have feelings, are proper objects of human love and devotion. In today's terms, pantheism is pretty much a platitude. But in orthodox Christian terms of 200 years ago, pantheism was an exciting and dangerous heresy.

Over 200 years since then, God has shrunk. He's lost most of his Kingdom, his Power and his Glory. Where once he parted oceans for the benefit of those who loved him, condemned his enemies to burning Hell, and deployed light itself in the course of four stunning chords of Haydn's *Creation*, he is now little more than a cosy feeling at Christmas. Meanwhile, as the clearing of a fallen redwood is invaded by creeping scrub and aspen, the business of landscape appreciation has grown to fill the hole.

The Christian position is this. God did not create

the natural world as a manifestation of Himself. He created the natural world for the use and amusement of mankind. Man then, through his tree-themed first sin of apple-eating, damaged that natural world. Orthodox Christianity, right into the 18th century, identified mountains specifically as part of that sin-sponsored damage. The original perfect world, of flat farmland and gardens, was wrecked by the sloshing waters of Noah's Flood.

As an English Romantic, the Wordsworth who stood on Snowdon at sunrise in 1791 was an atheist, and a lover of wild landscape. But the landscape love was more important than the atheism. By the time he died, 50 years later, he was combining the landscape love with an orthodox Anglicanism. This represents a sad decline in William Wordsworth. But also, a sad decline in Anglicanism.

John Muir followed a more honourable version of the Wordsworth trajectory. Quite abruptly, on his 1,000-mile walk, he abandoned the orthodox (in his case, Presbyterian) God.

He [God] is regarded as a civilised, law-abiding gentleman in favour of either a republic form of government or of a limited monarchy; believes in the literature and language of England, is a warm supporter of the English constitution and

Sunday schools and missionary societies, and is purely a manufactured article as any puppet of a halfpenny theatre.

In his later writings, God does get more than passing mention. But this new God of Muir's is high, indeed sky-piercing, ancient and sublime—but is also reddish-coloured at the base, sprouts branches higher up, and is in fact a sequoia tree.

Do behold the King in his glory, King Sequoia! Behold! Behold! seems all I can say. Some time ago I left all for Sequoia and have been and am at his feet; fasting and praying for light, for is he not the greatest light in the woods, in the world? Where are such columns of sunshine, tangible, accessible, terrestrialised?... I'm in the woods, woods, woods, and they are in me-ee-ee. The King tree and I have sworn eternal love—sworn it without swearing, and I've taken the sacrament with Douglas squirrel, drunk Sequoia wine, Sequoia blood, and with its rosy purple drops I am writing this woody gospel letter...

See Sequoia aspiring in the upper skies, every summit modelled in fine cycloidal curves as if pressed into unseen moulds, every bole warm in the mellow amber sun. How truly godful in mien!

Muir, as a grown-up, never attended the indoor sort of church. After his 1,000-mile walk he moved directly into the kind of pantheism that uses God as a short name for the feelings of love and awe inspired by the natural world: for the snowy sunrise on Half Dome, the storm spent in the top of the giant Douglas Fir.

Wishy-washy pantheism is the belief that, in some sense, everything that is, is God. It can be as little as the general niceness of it all, especially trees and flowers. Just as giving everybody the vote is much the same as giving nobody the vote, so the belief that everything is God is indistinguishable from the belief that nothing is. Which is just how John Scotus Erigena explained it to the Frankish king Charles the Bald in 840AD:

We do not know what God is. God himself doesn't know what He is because He is not anything.
Literally God is not, because He transcends being.

Serious and authentic pantheists go further than this—into an emotional involvement with rocks, stones, and vegetation. Fir cones and boulders are sentient, they have feelings. And we don't just love them, they love us right back.

This strict form of pantheism—God is the stones, and accordingly, stones have souls—this runs like a chain of small lakes through the nature writing of the last 200 years. It's there in Whitman's poem about the sequoia.

> *Perennial hardy life of me with joys 'mid rain*
> *and many a summer sun,*
> *And the white snows and night and the wild*
> *winds;*
> *O the great patient rugged joys, my soul's strong*
> *joys unreck'd by man,*
> *(For know I bear the soul befitting me, I too*
> *have consciousness, identity,*
> *And all the rocks and mountains have, and all*
> *the earth).*

It is explicit in John Muir.

> *Plants are credited with but dim and uncertain*
> *sensation, and minerals with positively none at*
> *all. But why may not even a mineral arrangement*
> *of matter be endowed with sensation of a kind*
> *that we in our blind exclusive perfection can have*
> *no manner of communication with?*

Pebbles do not have personality. They don't have a nervous system, they don't have hormones, there isn't anything there to have feelings with. It's we humans that have feelings. And our most powerful feelings are the sexual ones. We become passionate about, we love, some other human being. An important part of that is the feeling, communicated by small signals of the eyes and skin and smell, that the other human has similar feelings about us. Except by the student of body language, those signs are not consciously seen—and who loves the creepy Neuro-Linguistic Programming instructor? But sometimes, sadly, we love someone so much that we feel those responding signs are there when actually they aren't. Johnny Depp, Natalie Portman, that auburn-bearded, blue-eyed Mr Muir—they do not, in cold truth, reciprocate our passion. And neither do the trees and stones.

In the 1970s a zoologist (and sumo wrestling presenter) called Lyall Watson hooked a lie detector to his office pot plant and discovered that it responded with dismay to its fellow plants being tortured with lighted cigarettes in the next room. Watson spells his first name differently from the great geologist Charles Lyell who gave his name to the Lyell Canyon above Tuolumne. Watson's own science has proved unrepeatable. And given these uncertainties, it has to be better to direct your passions at a person, rather than a pebble.

Notes and references

p103 (epigraph) Andrew Marvell: 'To His Coy Mistress'.

p106 ('glorious region') John Muir: letter to *San Francisco Evening Bulletin,* 1875.

p109 (table) US National Park Service, as of December 2002.

p112 Walt Whitman: 'A Woman Waits for Me' in *Leaves of Grass.*

p113 ('I lay down the book') H D Thoreau: *Walden,* 1854.

p113 ('We have had many harbingers') R W Emerson: *The Transcendentalist,* 1842.

pp115–116 ('God is civilised') John Muir: *A Thousand Mile Walk to the Gulf,* 1867.

p116 ('King Sequoia') John Muir: letter to Mrs Ezra Carr, 1870s, dated 'Squirrelville, Sequoia Co. Nut Time'.

p118 ('Perennial hardy life') Walt Whitman: 'Song of the Redwood Tree' from *Leaves of Grass.*

p118 ('plants are credited') John Muir: *A Thousand Mile Walk to the Gulf.*

12 Palisades

Here among the mountains the pinions of thought should be strong, and one should see the errors of men from a calmer height of love and wisdom.

Emerson

 Le Conte Canyon gives us three hours through the forest; then we turn uphill along the Palisade Creek for an hour, so as to do some of tomorrow's uphill today. In the dusk, two fast walkers come up the trail.

'Nice camp site here,' I suggest quietly, so as not to startle them: in accordance with the research of Kevin Saunders (Chapter 5) they have not noticed us among the trees.

The two don't seem quite right together. The older is like Esau in the Bible: he is 'an hairy man' with worn-out equipment and untidy hair. The younger is like Jacob: he's a smooth man. Esau wants to march on into the darkness. Jacob the smooth man wants to stop.

The difference between them can be summarised: Jacob wears a moustache, but Esau a beard. When it comes to long distance hiking, facial hair is fundamental. The man with the moustache thinks of himself as a soldier. His outfit is well used but was originally very expensive. He lightens his pack by using, always, what is modern and complicated. If you look interested, he will tell you all about his equipment, where it came from, what it weighs, what it does, and the various other things it does in the submenu. He will do the same if you look completely bored. For the man with the moustache, the fun of hiking starts in the hiking shop. His GPS navigator is in a handy holster; he takes it out and cherishes its buttons like a teenager with her mobile phone.

The hiker with the big beard likes to think of himself as an old-time brigand—he hasn't spotted that real brigands are rarely pacifist and never vegetarian. His outfit is also well worn, but was bad even to begin with. Still, a bit of string will hold it together until Mount Whitney. What a shame, then, that he didn't bring any string…

John Muir went into the mountains with a tin cup tied to his belt on one side and a chunk of bread on the other. Stale bread was better than fresh as it didn't fall off the string. Muir didn't even put nails into his boots, not until he'd fallen over on the granite slabs a few times. Needless to say, Muir walked behind a beard. I'm a bearded walker myself, although because the beard is patchy and unattractive, I shave it off every few days before it can become outwardly visible. Henry David Thoreau's youthful chin-beard was straggly black, and was noted by women friends for its quite extraordinary unattractiveness. Even his favourite huckleberry was the wild, hairy one.

Henry David Thoreau

But when it comes to a walking comrade, two things are even more important than the facial hair. Those two things are the feet. How fast do they move along the trail, and how early or late in the morning do they start to do it? Many of the hikers we met were old enough to be on their second wives; and however much they may have been distracted on the first time around by personality, glamour or sexual prowess, the second time around they've selected on one crucial criterion. Why have a wife if she walks too slow, or even worse, too quickly?

Jacob the moustache set up camp one to the east of our tent, Esau the beard to the west. They are indeed walking together simply because of both being the same speed. Except that, as happens with two fast people, they've been going faster than that as each one tries to keep up with the other. They've come over from McClure Meadow—which we'd passed at lunchtime on the previous day—and six miles back, had passed Jim from Georgia already set up for the night. Esau gathered pine branches and soon we were enjoying the authentic High Sierra campfire experience. Jacob told us, with pride, that he'd acquired a trail name, 'Candyman', because of the confectionery he carries in net pockets outside his pack. Presumably he was flattered by the reference to the Christina Aguilera hit of the previous spring, where the sweet-talking, sugar coated candyman is 'a one-stop shop [who] makes the panties drop'. Does he know, though, that 'Candyman' is 1960s slang for a drug dealer?

In real life 'Jacob' is a computer systems analyst who planned a year out along with wife, but couldn't wait, and started without her three months early. He was walking from Lake Tahoe to Mount Whitney, a longer stint than merely the JMT. As he trekked he was tracking by their bootprints a group from Seattle he'd lost by stopping in at Vermilion.

Candyman was to bestow on us a joint trail name, the flattering 'Flying Scotsmen'—in admiration of the way we were going almost as quickly as himself. Esau his companion gazes quietly into the fire. An unsuccessful grocer, we gather, but not a great talker.

As the night closes in, and the firelight shines red on the tree trunks, Jacob offers around his 'Mountain House' blueberry cheesecake. It involves pouring hot water into three separate containers: a yellow firm-textured sludge (the biscuit), a pale slippery sludge (the topping) and a purple sugary sludge (the blueberry bit). 'Candyman' indeed! Though all this sophisticated cookery is a bit of a fiddle, and it would be just as delicious as a simple combination sludge in beige.

The next bit is the 'Golden Staircase', described as a path engineered out of a solid rock face. It's actually just more zigzags. Above is the Palisades Lake—blue, and surrounded by bare rock among big spiky mountains. The various lakes have their likeness, but each of the passes has its style and character. Mather Pass, this second 12,000-er, is as bleak as the Muir one was, but more sudden, with a narrow ridgeline, then a steep rocky drop to a moraine plain with more small lakes.

Five days earlier, at Vermilion, hiker Primrose had invited us to her 21st birthday party at Taboose Pass trail junction. Since then we had neither seen nor heard of Primrose and her friend Chanson. This was odd, as they should have overtaken us while we were at Muir Trail Ranch, and again as we ascended Mount Solomons.

Their ingenious plan: Primrose's Mom would come in over Taboose Pass, with food for their final four days plus, presumably, the birthday cake. We were early for the birthday rendezvous, but so were Primrose and Chanson—it turned out they'd mislaid themselves up various side trails. We spent a warm afternoon relaxing by the tarn. Esau the grocer arrived, without Jacob the Candyman. Jacob had been overdoing it and decided to take a stationary day. Primrose explained to us how she went to the discount hiking store on the day when they shift what didn't sell even at a discount, and so equipped herself from hat to unbranded trail shoes for under $50. We hadn't needed the explanation. One can see the face-hair on a hiker even when it isn't there: and not all of the 'bearded' sort of hikers are actually male.

A walker paused on the trail above, so I strolled up to see him.

'Is this Lake Marjorie, and have you seen four guys from Seattle?' It's Jacob the Candyman, supposedly on a day of not hiking at all.

In a normal small town, a nasty neighbour means you have to move away. On the trail, where everything shifts south-east at fifteen miles a day, you escape by standing still, or just by pretending to. Despite the matching speeds, the difference in facial hairstyles had turned out fundamental. Down at the lakeside, I didn't tell Esau that the moustached trail mate left behind him was now in fact in front.

The Mom scheme was not so ingenious after all. Taboose Pass is a climb of 6,000 feet, equivalent to two of the passes on the main trail on top of each other. Afternoon became evening and no Mom came. The sunset, flaming across the ridges of Mount Ruskin, had to do duty for the birthday candles.

'I'd like to offer them some food,' said Esau the grocer. 'But I'm down to the bare bones, me, just the bare bones.'

The breeze whispered through the dead grasses. Mountains turned black against the stars. Chanson filled her friend's tent with balloons, and we sang Happy Birthday.

'That Jacob the Candyman gave me some of this Mountain House food, I don't know why, I'm not carrying any stove, I'm down to the bare bones, me.'

We lent Esau a spell on our stove to cook his Mountain House. In Esau's opinion, Primrose and Chanson should keep going. People carry far too much food, you just have to ask them for it, it's doing them a favour really. Esau carried glucose powder, and trail mix bars. Come to think of it, maybe even those had been bummed off his better-equipped comrade, the Candyman. 'I love the man,' as Donovan sang in 1965: 'Yeah the Candy Man, he gets me high.' As for 'bummer', that was, originally, a raiding forager in General Sherman's march from Atlanta to the Sea: the 300-mile hike mentioned back in Chapter 11.

Next morning we left the two women some food that had been our spare supper in case we didn't quite cross Mount Whitney next Thursday, and that would get them out across the Taboose Pass. A short climb led to our next lovely lake. A walker with a moustache on stood at his camp and talked to us from a high rock above the trail.

'Was that Jacob up there?' Esau the grocer wondered, puzzled. We admitted that it had looked rather like him.

Above the high lake was the next high pass, the Pinchot. At its top, Esau caught us up again and pointed to grey streaky cloud on the skyline behind: 'It's not like what we've seen before, and it's bad.'

We recalled the hurricane warning of three days previously. It was now—careful counting on our fingers revealed—Monday. We could hope for two more trail days, and then presumably would be pulling out, the trail uncompleted, Mount Whitney unclimbed-up. The coming storm was a consolation for the girls behind, who wouldn't have finished the trail even with the Mom re-supply. But feeling dismal on our own account, we descended to Woods Creek. The aspens were yellowing, in what was presumably to be a two-day autumn before the coming winter storm.

Dismalness continued until Tom had a clever idea. Mount Whitney (the high point of the USA not counting Alaska) is quite close to Death Valley (its low point). Given two extra days of not crossing Mount Whitney, we'd hire ourselves a car and visit Death Valley instead.

As we approached Rae Lakes the trail got busier. We asked three of the trail parties, they having only recently left civilisation, what the weather forecast was. They said it would be sunny and delightful for ever and ever. And the clouds behind really hadn't been noticeably nasty. We decided to forget, for a second time, about the coming hurricane.

Are the Rae Lakes the loveliest of all the pine-scattered, crag-surrounded, waterside campsites? We had time to consider this question, as we arrived not quite early enough to continue over the next big climb, the Glen Pass. There were other things to think about too. I'd made a mistake with the schedule. With no need to stop anywhere in particular, I'd put the final 50 miles—to the base of Mount Whitney—at a sensible three days, and left it at that. But the three days, evenly divided, put us tomorrow night at the very crest of Forester Pass, 13,000 feet up. This was not a plausible campsite.

In front of us were Glen Pass, at 12,000 feet,

Forester Pass, at 13,000 feet, and then a long forest trek to Guitar Lake at the base of Mount Whitney. Today, as we'd already worked out, was Monday night. Buses leave Lone Pine on Fridays, and we had a plane to catch in LA on Saturday. The alternatives (for tired brains, this took time to determine):

• A short Tuesday tomorrow over Glen Pass to the base of Forester, then an eleven-hour Wednesday to Guitar Lake.

• An eleven-hour tomorrow over both Glen and Forester, then a gentle Wednesday to Guitar Lake.

As we'd spent so long thinking, we were now feeling quite fresh. So we went for the long Tuesday.

Notes and references

p121 (epigraph) R W Emerson: journal entry, 1832.

p123 Thoreau's beard: novelist Louisa May Alcott remarked to Emerson that the chin-beard 'will most assuredly deflect amorous advances and preserve the man's virtue in perpetuity'. Colman, William, et al, *The Journals and Miscellaneous Notebooks of Ralph Waldo Emerson* (Cambridge, Mass 1960–). HDT lived in chastity by his own choice and conviction, though the bad beard must have helped.

13 Forester Pass

Almost the whole of it had been fashioned with no other tool than a jack-knife. It would record the seconds, minutes, hours, day of the week and day of the month; and it had an apparatus attached by a light cord to a delicate set of levers at the foot of his bed. The frame of the bed was hung on trunnions; and, at a desired hour the clock would release a catch and the sleeper be tilted to nearly a standing posture.

Harvey Reid on John Muir's wake-up system

On 12th May, 1998, Stephen Venables came down from the summit of Everest. At the South Col he rejoined his two companions who, too ill and exhausted to attempt the summit, had spent the day there among the abandoned oxygen bottles, wrecked tents, and corpses left by earlier expeditions.

They had reached the South Col by the difficult and dangerous Kangshung Face. Next morning they began their preparations for setting off back down it. Still in their sleeping bags they lit their stoves. In the low pressure the stoves burned fitfully, but eventually they made tea, and melted enough snow to fill their water bottles for the day. They drank the tea.

Then it was time to start putting their boots on. One at a time (there were three in one small tent) they wriggled out of their sleeping bags, removed gloves, and struggled with the boot fastenings. Although only their half-frozen fingers were actually moving, they still were breathing like long-distance runners in the thin air. At 7,900 metres there is not enough air to sustain life. The aim of any Everest climber is to be moving quickly enough, and dying slowly enough, to get down before getting dead. These three had been up here, dying, for three days, and their movements were slowing. Having got all six boots on, they left the tent and looked at the tent pegs. They looked at their watches. It was already afternoon. It wasn't worth taking down the tent. They took their boots off, and got back inside the tent.

The following morning, with a greater appreciation of the urgency of their case, they managed successfully to strike camp and set off down the Kangshung Face.

My friend and advisor Ian planned his JMT trip with his wife of 30 years, and trail comrade over the same period. Another couple, friends for almost as long, asked to join them. They set off as a party of six—with only a single, joint, trail permit.

For two of the party, this was a long-awaited and very special holiday. On holiday, you don't get up early; you enjoy a nice lie-in. And then you sit in the sun. And you forgot your lip balm, you unpack your rucksack and get out your lip balm. And on one morning, the business of hitting the trail took four and a half hours. This did not result in anybody's death. What it resulted in was walking through the very hottest part of the day, without rest breaks. The further result was cooking and camping in the dark. But it didn't lead to death—not even to anybody's murder.

'We are all still friends,' Ian assures me. 'And we did enjoy the trip, don't think we didn't.'

Tom and I have been trekking together since he was sixteen. That Dads are not infallible was an early and important lesson—and one that, after the leaky groundsheet and underwater awakening at Angle Tarn, did not need to be repeated. But was, later that day, when the path across to Ravenglass turned out tidal and under twenty feet of the sea. At the age of four, Tom believed that the BBC transmitted the chimes of Big Ben at 6pm to indicate to infants of Britain the time for being in bed. He no longer believes that. But he does still believe the idea that trail days start at first light, and that, one hour afterwards, you should be on the move.

Mature Americans we met on the trail had divorced their first wives to find new ones that matched their own trail speed. But have I committed a worse eugenic? Raising a son to fit my own ideals of campcraft...

Our routine is to rise at first light, which in September is 6am; to enjoy a chilly and not very enjoyable breakfast; and hit the trail just as the sun rises. This lets us enjoy the cool of the day walking, cover 15 miles without any hurry and with a one-hour lunch of peanut butter crackers, and then enjoy lounging at some lakeside through several hours of the hot bit at the day's ending. But for this long day we rose in the starlight at 5am, and hit the trail at first light. Glen Pass was a pile of multi-coloured rubble, with a weirdly striped mountain overhead, and (thankfully) the usual good path underfoot. Sunrise struck us at the pass top. Thus we had all morning for the long trek through the trees of bear-infested Bubbs Creek to the base of Forester Pass.

High above and far away, jagged mountains closed off the valley head. The trail rose, the creek diminished, the trees became more sparse. The trail passed up through scrub, and lunch was a last green patch at a pool surrounded by stones. The trail zigzagged through the stones to the sterile grey-blue lake below Junction Peak.

The Americans we met along the trail were very companionable and charming, as they pointed out that John Muir was Scottish like us, claimed their Scottish ancestor, and proudly displayed their approximate knowledge of where Scotland was, before apologising for George W Bush. The couple enjoying the sight of Junction Peak were at least as charming as everybody else. But after ten minutes and more, they still hadn't apologised for George W. Instead, they were telling us interesting items about Junction Peak, and precisely how hard it would have been to go up it if we'd been wanting to. Class 3, but with one move that might be Class 5. Looking up at it from the tarn, the ridge stood against the sky like a big blunt granite saw-blade. (And *sierra*, sawblade, is what some inaugural Mexican saw when he looked this way.) To reach even the beginning of the ridge, you'd have already come at least two days with your tent, and have climbed to the highest pass on the John Muir Trail, and (unless you'd started the thing properly, from Yosemite) be suffering quite severely from the altitude.

The path worked ever upwards among the great boulderfields (American 'talus') below the closing crags. A dozen final zigzags led to the crest. 13,180 feet is, for the cosmopolitan, just about 4,020 metres—

Junction Peak

and at 13,180 feet altitude it took me fifteen minutes to make the calculation in my head. This was my first time at such height since Mont Blanc 35 years ago; Tom's first time ever.

The descent from Forester is a crag-cut pathway with big drops below it. A yellow-bellied marmot grabbed one of the sparse trailside plants and sat on a stone gnawing at it. It knew we were waiting to grab its sparse plant but kept its eye on us so we couldn't. The rock-cut path slanted into talus, and ran down to another high, stony valley.

We headed towards the distant forest. It had been a long day, and we wanted to stop. However, after its initial exciting drop to 12,000 feet the path descends only gradually. Every 500 feet of height loss was going to make the coming night that much less bitter, but at the cost of an hour of extra walking now. But the couple at Junction Tarn had kindly pinpointed for us their favourite camp: at the foot of the very highest tree-belt, and a half-mile down off the path. And it was a beauty. It was in a slight valley hollow, which was why the trees were there in the first place, further sheltered by the trees themselves, and with a selection of tent squares already cleared of rocks and pebbles. Out of courtesy to our hosts, we chose the second nicest tent-square. Through the last few trees, it looked along a meadow that still showed a tinge of green among its autumn yellow grasses. The meadow stream ran just below us, over golden stones between banks of aromatic shrubs.

Two men came crashing down through the trees to join us. One was a teenage stockbroker enjoying his first five days away in three years (well, all right, he was in his mid-twenties). And the couple who'd sent all four of us down to intrude on their favourite camp ground were obliged to take a bitterly cold site just out of the tree shelter. But they weren't too worried, as they had really effective air-filled sleeping mattresses.

After we'd finished admiring the sleeping mattresses, we found out that the kindly couple were from Texas, with all that implies in terms of good-natured friendliness, an accent you could fry eggs over, supporting G W Bush, and enthusiastic gun ownership (though not within the national park, happily). He was a former pro-football player and still big and strong; she smaller but tough. After a life in business, he was semi-retired, and had set up his own NGO (non-government organisation, what we'd call Voluntary Sector) with the aim of placing a bible preacher in every one of the 51 state capitals (twenty done, the rest to come, and then Europe...)

The underaged broker explained how a colleague had taken a holiday a few weeks back, and the market had made its 'correction' of August 2007 (otherwise known as the abrupt collapse at the beginning of the sub-prime mortgage fiasco) and the man had lost half his clients just by not being there twenty-four-stroke-seven. But even so, you have to have a holiday sometimes, can't wait until early retirement at 35 to take time on the trail. His Significant Other had bought him a canister of bear Mace (tear gas) and where were the lakes with the fish in?

Bible Man told of distant unvisited lakes, tucked under the high peaks, where trout were like tuna fish. We spoke of Scotland, and warned that it was a place where it quite often is raining. We all told where we'd been on the trail and where we were going to go. The sun nipped in behind the nearby mountaintop and the temperature went from chilly to a lot colder than that. The Bible couple lit a fire. The stockbroker spoke again of his Significant Other—was this gender-unspecific term a way of discreetly not revealing that the SO was, in fact, a chap?

Writing in the *Independent on Sunday* about Jérôme Kerviel, the rogue trader who in 2008 lost five billion euros belonging to his employers, the Société Générale, Oliver James cited a study of New York brokers as showing that

> *On average they spent twelve hours a day at work, smoked nearly two packs of cigarettes, consumed alcohol and some form of illegal substance (mostly cocaine) twice a day. For relaxation they chose solitary pursuits: jogging, masturbation and fishing more often than dining with friends or sex with others.*

Our fireside companion had broken that trend, and it was quite unfair that his short break was about to be shortened further by uncontrollable weather conditions, whereupon he was going to discover that the second and more serious stage of credit crunch had been happening without him.

We sat with hot fronts and cold backs, with the firelight on our faces and the mountains black against the stars. A few feet behind us, the dry grass was already crisp with frost. (Muir had been there before us. In 1875 he ascended Mount Shasta in mid-winter, and was trapped overnight on the summit, in a blizzard. He hadn't been expecting the blizzard, and had left his overcoat lower down to save carrying the weight of it... All night long, in his shirtsleeves, he warmed himself at one of the fumaroles, hot steam vents in the crater of Mount Shasta. The zone of comfort, between singed front and frozen behind, must have been mere millimetres.)

From out of the darkness, Bible Man had a question to ask. 'You and this Significant Other—are you planning on getting married, then?' The broker claimed that marriage was, indeed, their intention. And his friend, once he'd got a bit further with his career, yes, he was meaning to get married as well.

And me, and Thomas's mother? Had I been married to her, was I indeed still? This question did not in fact come... And I was fairly sure, from hints in their discourse, that the marriage-touting pair were in fact both pre-divorced. And presumably remarried to each other on the important criterion of trail-speed matching.

All evening, the jingly lyrics and tune of the Christmas song wouldn't get out of my head. Subliminally at some moment I must have hummed them: for Thomas, too, found himself infected with the idea of building a snowman in a meadow, and pretending it's the preacher-man: 'He'll say are you married we'll say no, man; but you can do the job while you're in town...'

Notes and references

p132 (epigraph) According to Badè's biography, Muir's self-awakening bed only did this if the sleeper was correctly aligned in bed. Otherwise it bumped him out onto the floor. It was described by Harvey Reid, a fellow student at Wisconsin, in *Outlook* magazine, 1903. As Siegfried Giedion points out in *Mechanisation Takes Command* (1948), the American Mid-west in the 1860s produced more inventions per head of population than anywhere else, ever. Ingenious farmers with land but no labour first redesigned all basic tools such as scythe and axe. They then devised machines like the self-binding reaper which, powered only by its own wheels dragging on the ground, assembles a wheatsheaf, knots and cuts the string around it, and ejects it onto the ground.

p142 The song is 'Winter Wonderland' by Dick Smith and Felix Bernard, from 1934.

14 Mount Whitney

*Like love affairs, expeditions usually continue just
a little too long. The end is always a little rueful,
and tinged with impatience.*

Richard Fortey

*My body of a sudden blazed;
and twenty minutes, more or less
it seemed, so great my happiness
That I was blessed, and could bless.*

W B Yeats

 In a piece about the UK's mountain rocks
I described the dull ocean-bottom sludges
that formed the Southern Uplands. And
then I wrote that volcanic rocks made a
better sort of mountain, in Snowdonia
and the Lake District. I knew this was dodgy, and
sure enough my editor crossed out 'better' and wrote
'higher' instead.

Anything that could be disagreed with is a 'value
judgement'. Substitute a fact, however boring that
fact may be. So, on naming a mountain, its altitude
(14,495 feet) is to be placed in brackets after. If

the mountain is of particular significance, then its altitude will be given also in the metric system (14,495 feet/4,421 metres). And certain landmark facts, like gnarled signposts, appear at their particular place in the trail. Helen and Wanda Lakes are named for John Muir's two daughters—this is so much simpler than trying to describe them. Say that Wanda Lake is sterile—and someone might suggest that actually it has some interesting protozoans, so insert 'comparatively', adding some single-celled protozoans to Wanda but taking all the life out of your assertion? Say that Wanda Lake is ugly—oh now you're being judgemental. So say that it's named after Muir's daughter. And if we want a bit of vivid detail to liven up the story: well, add the lassie's date of birth.

So when I write of Mount Whitney (14,495 feet), I hasten to mention that it is the highest point in the contiguous USA. Here, of course, we exclude Mount McKinley (OK, Denali, but don't get me started on the cult of obscurantist but 'authentic' hill names) which is unpleasantly steep and snowy and totally lacks trail signposts and ranger stations. But, within the 'contiguous' USA, is Mount Whitney (14,480 feet) thus, necessarily, the best?

Altitude does matter. Everest (8,850 metres) is a more interesting hill than Kinder Scout (638 metres).

While Clouds Rest (9,926 feet) may be a very pleasant place, Mount Whitney (14,495 feet) will almost certainly be a more challenging and worthwhile ascent. Even so, not necessarily. The most popular Polish mountain is Giewont, the Sleeping Knight— despite its being 604 metres lower than Poland's high point at Rysy (2,498 metres). Rysy is overlooked by Gerlachovsky stit (2,655 metres) which happens to be in Slovakia. But Giewont stands proud and alone at the northern edge of the Tatras. From the plains of Poland, it presents a jagged and exciting outline— the sleeping knight still has his beaked metal helmet on. And when you get onto it, it's rocky but not too rocky, a chain-assisted scramble with quite a bit of exposure, not like that damned Denali (sorry, did I forget to put it in last time—Denali, 20,320 feet). A fortnight waiting out a blizzard in an ice-cave floored with human excrement: this is more seriousness than we want in a National High Point. Also, there are grizzly bears. So thank the god of tall things for that weasely 'contiguous'.

In the Lake District, the top tops are, in altitude terms, just slightly lower. A pre-glacial erosion surface forms the very highest summits, and Scafell, Great Gable and Helvellyn are all flat on top. Sharp-edged Steeple stands 73 feet below, but so much higher in esteem, than the erosion surface of Great Scoat Fell. Of Scotland's hills, the highest with an exciting sharp-ridged summit is Carn Mor Dearg, number six in the list. Mont Blanc is a fine mountain: its immense size allows lots and lots of rock and ice, airy ridges, and interesting outliers. But its summit is a snowfield with a couple of hundred people standing around eating sandwiches. The Matterhorn, 332 metres lower down, is even more of a mountain than Mont Blanc. And Whitney's broad plateau, which actually has a hut on, looks down from its superior position (at the very top of the contiguous US) on Junction Peak. Junction Peak's mere 13,888 feet have been carved by glaciers to below the erosion plateau, and it rises in three rocky ridges to a tiny pointed top. One of the three glaciers is still there, even, all covered over with boulder stones. For my money, and even though I haven't been up it yet, Junction Peak looks like the top summit of the Sierra. Just how hard, please, is a 'Class 3 with a few moves of Class 5'?

An ancestral cousin of mine, Ronald William Turnbull Hudson, was described in the account of the accident as a 'very valuable' life lost in Snowdonia's Devil's Kitchen. As well as being distinguished as only the second climber to lose his life in Wales, he was first in his year as a Cambridge mathematician, and author of a definitive (but posthumous) text on Kummel's Quartic Surface. But today we wouldn't say that about him. It's axiomatic that all lives are equally very valuable. Hills, too? That is the instinct of my editor (though he did add a query to his correction, inviting a less tendentious assertion such as that Snowdonia is 'more rugged' than the Southern Uplands.) Thus Clouds Rest is indeed of equal merit with Mount Whitney. Scafell (964 metres) is equally deserving with Great Sca Fell (651 metres) at the back o' Skiddaw. Great Sca's lack of spectacular crags and airy ridges is counterbalanced by its lack of crowds. Or, as one over-enthusiastic outdoor writer put it: 'At the Back o' Skiddaw you'll meet more sheep than people, and the walkers wear smiles of quiet satisfaction.'

It's a simple but satisfying equation. Because Great Sca Fell is so boring, hardly anybody goes there. Because hardly anybody goes there, that actually makes it even better than all the other hills where everybody does go. And as for all the folk on Scafell —they are far outnumbered by all the folk on its less exciting outlier Scafell Pike (978 metres).

Because it's a ~~better~~ higher hill. All right?

With the lazy Wednesday ahead, we lie in until 7am, and bumble down the valley taking arty photos.

Two hours later, an approaching hiker brings news from the ranger station. Remember that hurricane warning we already forgot about twice? Well, it was spot on. It's going to start snowing tonight, and the big storm is tomorrow morning. We have just crossed the 13,000-foot Forester Pass, and ahead of us is the 13,500-foot Trail Crest pass that's alongside Whitney summit. And although I have insurance against being rescued by helicopter, Tom doesn't.

Well now, just how far away is Whitney? If we started walking rather fast—and didn't stop for peanut butter and crackers but ate chewy bars on the move —and carried on walking rather fast—perhaps we might reach Trail Crest by 4pm. If we did, then we'd have two hours for up and down Whitney, and an hour down the back in the general direction of Lone Pine before being benighted. Unless we got tired, or the altitude hit our lungs, or the cloud came down below 13,000 feet, or the storm came early. (But in the end, it's not the problems you worry about in advance that knock you down; it's the one you didn't even consider…)

We walked rather fast and didn't stop for lunch. Wispy cirrus came from behind us and started filling the sky. The ranger at the ranger station said that the snow wasn't going to start until tomorrow; but, on the other hand, it was gusting 50mph on Whitney summit right now. Well, how's about that? We can go up to Trail Crest and then straight down to Lone Pine. But if we get to Trail Crest by 4pm, and we aren't too tired, and the altitude hasn't hit our lungs, and the cloud hasn't come down below 13,000 feet, and the storm hasn't arrived, *and* the wind isn't too strong—then we'll make a try for Mount Whitney (unless we get prevented by that one problem we haven't even considered). The ranger agreed that this was a reasonable plan.

We came out of the trees to Guitar Lake. Back in the north, we could see the mountains gathering cloud around their summits. Overhead, the cirrus now covered the sky, and the thicker stratus was creeping up behind it. Long, long switchbacks led up the craggy side of Mount Whitney to the trail junction below the Trail Crest pass. To be here, 4pm was the last sensible time. It was, at this moment, 3pm. Heading up Whitney wasn't merely possible. It was actually the sensible thing to do.

The ridge to Whitney is narrow and rocky, with huge vertical drops on the Lone Pine side but drops that are merely steep and fairly huge on the side where we were. In Scotland, the ridge to Whitney would be a sporting scramble, not unlike the Aonach Eagach but with even further to fall. In the Alps, the ridge to Whitney would be a sporting scramble marked out with paint spots and protected with a fixed chain. But this is the US, and the ridge to Whitney is a cleverly-engineered terraced path, wide enough for people to pass, suitable for a mule. We weren't at all disgusted at this disparagement of the mountain. It was bitterly cold, and the wind wasn't 50mph but it was blustery enough to be disconcerting, and there was no engineering away the 2,000-foot slope dropping to our left.

We set off up the terraced path. And at that moment, the unforeseen problem that we hadn't even thought about—it didn't happen. So we still don't know what it would have been. An hour after everyone else had left it, we reached the summit of Mount Whitney.

There used to be 92 switchbacks in the path down from Trail Crest. They rebuilt it a bit, and now there are 96. I suspect they're going for the full hundred —there certainly are far more than you actually need when you're trying to head downhill quickly to get below the really chilly bits of the hill before night falls. Six thousand feet of downhill can be extremely trying, when you're tired and have sore and damaged feet. But after fifteen days of dry socks all the time,

Pinnacle on Mount Whitney

our feet were fine; and we were feeling fit. Indeed, we had the feeling of going on strongly, and being ready to go on going strongly. It kicks in, only when you're really fit, at the end of a really long hard day; so I don't know how the poet Yeats managed to get it sitting in a London coffee-shop. Endorphin surge or vision of Eternity, the feeling is an illusion that can collapse suddenly, but it is very pleasurable while it lasts, and for us it lasted until nightfall. At which point we cosily camped at about the 10,000-foot level (Outpost Camp) in sheltering trees well below the windswept stony zone.

Fortey the fossil-hunter, quoted at the top of the chapter, says that a long walk is like a love affair. In which case, we were getting out just before the big bust-up. Next morning, as we trekked gently down to the car-park, the first little snowflakes of the coming Winter Wonderland fell onto the path. Far back above, Mount Whitney was snow-white screeslopes running up into swirly cloud.

Notes and references

p143 (epigraph) Richard Fortey, paleontologist, spending two months on a shingle beach at Hinlopenstretet (80°N, between Spitzbergen and Nordauslandet) gathering fossil ammonites with a tent mate he didn't particularly like, 1967.

p143 (epigraph) W B Yeats: 'Vacillation'.

p147 ('Back o' Skiddaw') Quoted, unattributed, on Radio 4's The News Quiz. I shall not attempt to discover which of my colleagues wrote it.

15 Lone Pine

There are two sorts of starvation. Normal malnutrition—it should not be normal, it should be swept off the face of Earth—is when one has simply not had enough food. Recovery is slow, starting with sips of water with salt and glucose. The other—far less serious, and usually voluntary—is where one has enough food, but far too much exercise. Taking in 3,000 calories while burning up 5,000 gives the same shortfall as someone eating no food at all; the same sunken eyes and bony appearance. The difference is that we have had all the vitamins and minerals out of those 3,000 calories of food. Apart from being starved, we are tremendously healthy.

And so, once standing still in a place with food at it, we suffer a gross and embarrassing eating experience. Extreme athlete Dr Mike Stroud, whose book *Survival of the Fittest* explains these two sorts of starvation, spent several weeks hauling sledges across the Antarctic. He then found himself in Punta Arenas, the main town of Tierra del Fuego. He strolled down the main street until he found a hamburger bar, went in, and had a large hamburger. He strolled down the street until he found another hamburger bar, where he had another large hamburger. And so on, right across Punta Arenas.

I have experienced this sort of starvation on trains heading south out of the Scottish Highlands: going through the rucksack for overtravelled Mars bars, bent by body-heat, the corners of their wrappers rubbed away. And once, the gluttony struck at a sandwich supper arranged by the local choral society after a performance of Mozart's *Coronation Mass*. The choir members provide a surplus of sandwiches, in traditional flavours such as date with banana or Branson and ham. As inconspicuously as possible, I devoured seventeen sandwiches, hitting on the less popular combinations: cucumber and Marmite, cabbage in yellow vinegar.

For sufferers from this embarrassing eating condition, Lone Pine is the place to be. Lone Pine is not just western, but Western. The wide street separates two lines of low-rise diners, motels and hardware stores, all with false fronts slapped up hastily out of cardboard. Past the thrift shop and the final filling station, the long straight road heads out to nowhere. At the ends of the short side-streets are the Alabama hills, lumps of black basalt with a few wind-tortured plants. The Alabama Hills, once you've sorted out that they aren't in Alabama but are named after a Confederate battleship of the Civil War, are still spatially dislocated in the downwards direction. They belong to the very top of the Sierra, as we saw at Wanda Lake. The Sierra faultline has sunk them to within easy reach of the cocktail bars and swimming pools of Owens Valley, four hours drive from Los Angeles. And with the highest mountain in the contiguous USA as a handy backdrop, many a fine young American film star has been struck down in a pool of tomato ketchup in these wild (but only 1,000 feet high) Alabama Hills.

But one name of them all lives on in Lone Pine. The researcher Chuck Shepherd published a list of 883 murderers, or men charged with murder, with the middle name Wayne. Shepherd (who edits the online *News of the Weird*) suggests that what he has measured is a tendency for the kind of 1960s Dad who greatly admired 'The Duke' to father and raise boys who in later life become killers. In the Dow Motel, we sit surrounded on four walls by John Wayne. For variety, every tenth picture shows not Wayne himself but his love interest, or alternatively his horse.

And our main occupation in Lone Pine: to eat like a cowboy. Or, to be blunt about it, like his horse. The killer cowboy breakfast involves waffles, maple syrup, grits, eggs over easy (rather than the British equivalent, eggs in greasy), and shredded bacon. An American delicacy is biscuits with gravy. The biscuits are what we call scones, slightly sweet and raised with soda. The gravy is just gravy, sticky and pale grey. We pass a couple of hours in the laundromat and the souvenir shop; and then it's time for the killer cowboy lunch. We choose the healthy option: same as breakfast, but with a salad.

As we were enjoying our third cowboy-killer meal of the day, in came Primrose (now five days into maturity as a 21 year-old adult) and Chanson, along with the missing Mom. They'd crossed Whitney in the start of the snow, finding it no more than ankle-deep, so presumably we could have done so too. But the JMT is a path that's outstandingly beautiful, that gives good company along the trail, that among the granite has some stimulatingly visible geology —but is (whisper it softly) slightly too pleasant and straightforward. That last day of suspense and serious high-speed travel added necessary excitement and energy.

And with all that energetic walking to beat the snowstorm, we were a day ahead. So we hired a car, and went to Death Valley anyway.

16 New York

Once, the woods of America went on for ever. Thoreau could walk from Walden westwards, for days and weeks until he ran out of beans and a bear ate him up. But after changing planes at Philadelphia, we flew north above a hundred miles of suburbs. The pools were swimming-pools, and the only grassland was golf. Outbound, the plane had circled above Yosemite. Now, it circled to let us look along the artificial canyons of New York.

In 1868, John Muir got as far into New York as the piers along the East River. 'Often I thought I would like to explore the city if, like a lot of wild hills and valleys, it was clear of inhabitants.' Of particular interest was Central Park, designed ten years earlier by Frederick Law Olmsted. Olmsted had been chairman of the Yosemite Commission, which in 1864 first induced President Lincoln to protect and fund Yosemite as a state reserve. Olmsted created Central Park not as a place of prettiness, but as a rectangle of wild country within the city.

> *The time will come when New York will be built up, when all the grading and filling will be done, and when the picturesquely-varied, rocky formations of the Island [of Manhattan] will have been converted into formations for rows of monotonous straight streets, and piles of erect buildings. There will be no suggestion left of its present varied surface, with the single exception of the few acres contained in the Park. Then the priceless value of the present picturesque outlines of the ground will be more distinctly perceived...*
> *It therefore seems desirable to interfere with its easy, undulating outlines, and picturesque, rocky scenery as little as possible.'*

'Up in the Sierra, all along the gorges, the glaciers have put up natural signposts, and you can't miss your way, but here—there's nothing to tell you where to go,' Muir explained after getting lost in a San Francisco hotel. And when it came to Manhattan's wilderness, 'fearing that I might not be able to find my way back, I dared not make the adventure'. Braver than Muir, or just with a better map, I found my way to Central Park. Here are rock climbs, several metres high, on sparkly mica schist. In Yosemite, the pines grow tall where the bedrock lies deeply buried under glacier till. In Manhattan, it's the other way around. At either end of the island, where the firm grey schist lies close to the surface, there the skyscrapers can rise high. Central Park, where the schist is exposed in glacier-scraped sparkly humps, would be prime skyscraper terrain save for the stubbornness of Frederick Law Olmsted. Even while Muir failed to navigate the wild places of New York, Olmsted was threatening to resign as Park Superintendent in the face of schemes of prettiness as well as a low-budget zoo. He was finally dismissed in 1877.

From Sheep Meadow (where the sheep were actually people, drowsing in the hot afternoon) I adventured into the canyons of Manhattan. Having waited for the pedestrian signal, I strode briskly to mid-street, took my photo of the high confining walls, then scarpered before the flash flood of yellow cabs came surging down the canyon floor. 'No hooting except for anger,' exhorted a witty roadside sign (a letter D having been scratched from the final word); and a self-parodying New York driver leaned from his car window, shaking a fist, and yelling: 'Where's your coy-tesy? Hey, hey, where's your coy-tesy?'

The walls of Yosemite have stood for ten thousand years—and they are still, in rock-years, very young. The skyscrapers are historic: these walls of concrete and steel have stood for almost a century. It is not self-evident that they will stand for another one. In what is perhaps the most thoughtful and terrifying account of where the world is heading, Jared Diamond asks:

Will tourists someday stare mystified at the rusting hulks of New York's skyscrapers, much as we stare today at the jungle-overgrown ruins of Maya cities? ... It has long been suspected that many of those mysterious abandonments [Minoan Crete and Mycenean Greece, Great Zimbabwe, Easter Island] were at least partly triggered by ecological problems: people inadvertently destroying the environmental resources on which their societies depended.

From the futures trader on the 40th floor, right down to the beggars and prostitutes at street level, there's not a soul in this brash busy city but earns a virtual living, a living mediated by the belief system we call money. And while we were crossing the high passes of the Sierra, Britain for the first time in a century had experienced a run on one of our major banks, the so-called Northern Rock. Cash itself is disembodied into pulses within a computer.

New York

The system is so rapid and efficient that it can crash apart and collapse in milliseconds; reducing futures traders, street people, and outdoor writers alike to the fundamentals of food, shelter, and clothes. Of which I was in want of the third category. All that I had, I had worn or carried for two hundred miles across the mountains. Stuff for the journey home had not been part of the package.

I took my cash and credit card to the second-hand shops of Brooklyn. During the subway ride civilisation did not collapse; and for $25 I purchased three shirts, eight socks, and some city shoes.

Notes and references

p157 (epigraph) Byron: *Childe Harold's Pilgrimage,* canto 3, stanza 72 (1812–18).

p157 ('clear of inhabitants') John Muir: *A Thousand Mile Walk to the Gulf,* Chapter 8.

p158 ('The time will come') F L Olmsted and Calvert Vaux: 'Conception of the Plan', submitted to the New York City Commissioners c 1857.

p158 ('natural signposts') 'John Muir as I knew him': Robert Underwood Johnson, 1916, recalling his first meeting with Muir in 1889.

p160 J Diamond: *Collapse: How Societies Choose to Fail or Survive,* 2005, Introduction.

17 The Eagle in his Ink

Two roads diverged in a yellow wood ...
In leaves no step had trodden black...
Two roads diverged in a wood, and I—
I took the one less travelled by,
And that has made all the difference.

Frost

If you think about all the gains our society has
made, from independence to now, it wasn't
government. It was activism. People think, 'Oh,
Teddy Roosevelt established Yosemite National
Park, what a great president.' BS [Bullshit]. It was
John Muir who invited Roosevelt out and then
convinced him to ditch his security and go camping.
It was Muir, an activist, a single person.

Yvon Chouinard

Life is a long-distance walk. A clear view from the ridge-top of early adulthood: shop floor for the first ten years, stiff uphill section to the executive desk job and the six-cylinder car, at age 55 a glamorous mistress or toy boy, cottage in the mountains and first minor heart attack, and about 60 years from now a dignified death surrounded by seventeen grandchildren, three of whom have been named after us in hopes of a big slice of our millionaire estate...

A New Englander like Robert Frost sees it rather differently. Life is a long-distance walk—a long-distance walk in the woods. Life's an Appalachian Trail, where you never see more than a few steps ahead. The trail divides. The two paths may rejoin around the back of the big Douglas Fir. Or one way may lead to open yellow meadows beside the creek, and a view to the grey mountains and the pass high ahead: the other way, deeper into the trees.

But let a small log fall across that left-hand way, or erect a temporary signpost. The hikers all head to the right; that left-hand trail becomes mossed over and green, then lost under those slippery, curved needles of the sugar pine. And soon it becomes invisible. The slight bend that was once a forking point is now not even noticed; the route on the right appears as the simple straight trail. The road not taken fades, and becomes just another part of the undergrowth.

The poet Walt Whitman can be seen in a direct progression between Wordsworth (who first formulated in words the idea of a national park) and Muir (who made the idea a reality). But in fact Whitman stands at a forking of the trail. Use and passage has taken, always after Whitman, the direction of Muir, and the conservation of the wilderness. So that now, that line—from Wordsworth, through to Thoreau, and on to John, the Sierra Club, and the tree-hugger Julia Butterfly Hill sitting in the sequoia—that line appears as being, and having been always, the main straight trail.

In reality, Whitman's 'Song of the Redwood Tree' is a pro-logging poem.

With crackling blows of axes sounding musically driven by strong arms,
Riven deep by the sharp tongues of the axes, there in the redwood forest dense,
I heard the mighty tree its death-chant chanting.
The great trees die gladly, making way for an even nobler creation:
A swarming and busy race settling and organizing everywhere,
Ships coming in from the whole round world, and going out to the whole world,
To India and China and Australia and the thousand island paradises of the Pacific,
Populous cities, the latest inventions, the steamers on the rivers, the railroads, with many a thrifty farm, with machinery,

*And wool and wheat and the grape, and diggings
of yellow gold.*

Civilisation and the frontier, the bean-field and
the huckleberry, the bear and the big people-crusher
car. No contradiction, so long as there is the semi-
infinite sweep of the trees westwards. But in 1852,
the Californians from the west collided with the
Americans from the east, along the line of the Sierra
Nevada. The wilderness was no longer limitless.

History and tradition are on the side of the
American as entrepreneur. The lumberjack of the
frontier, the pioneer farmer with his axe and his
plough. (Or, get it right, his ax and his plow.) The
Texas oilman and the concrete canyons of New York
City. But at the branch-point of the two roads stood,
at the one important moment, John Muir from
Dunbar.

John Muir never intended himself as an activist.
For his first seven years in the Sierras, the absent
glaciers were far more important than the logging
companies slicing into the foothills. But his women
friends, unable to tidy up his frayed shirts and near-
dreadlocked hair, could at least rearrange his long,
ardent letters for publication as they flowed from
his eagle-feather quill pen. And in 1889 he guided
through Yosemite Mr Robert Underwood Johnson,

editor of *Century* magazine. Johnson asked him to write for a campaign for national park status for Yosemite. Muir was incredulous that he could make any difference; but wrote two articles anyway. They were published in August 1890; Johnson meanwhile was lobbying the Congress. The Yosemite Bill was signed into law six weeks later.

For the rest of his life, Muir's writing was politically motivated. And although his invitation to Ralph Waldo Emerson was turned down, in 1903 a far more impressionable and influential guest dropped into his granite-walled open air Bed & Breakfast.

In Autumn 1902, President Theodore Roosevelt needed to settle the border between Mississippi and Louisiana, and decided to combine a site visit with sport in the form of a bear hunt. Unfortunately, nobody told the bears, and they failed to show up. So the presidential guide lurked at a watering hole until a 235lb black bear cub happened along. He clubbed it over the head, tied it to a tree, and invited the president to take a shot.

This seemed to Roosevelt unsporting, particularly in the presence of the press. His not shooting of the bear was recorded in a cartoon, 'Drawing the Line in Mississippi', in the *Washington Post*. The president is shown in the slouch hat and uniform of the Rough Riders, turning his back on a cute cub with ears five times the usual size.

A hitherto unsuccessful toymaker called Morris Michtom recreated the unshot cub in brown plush, stuffed with excelsior and finished with black button eyes. (In other versions of the story, the stuffed Teddy entrepreneur is named as Richard Steiff.) The bear's special selling point was its realistically bendy arms and legs. Its other special selling point was that the president allowed it to be identified as 'Teddy's bear'. Meanwhile the real bear cub, injured by the hunting dogs, had been humanely killed by having its throat cut.

It was the following year, as the first 10,000 Teddy bears were stitched together, that Roosevelt offered himself a more authentic woodland adventure. 'I do not want anyone with you,' he wrote to John Muir; 'and I want to drop politics absolutely for four days, and just be out in the open with you.' Muir postponed a prearranged trip to Siberia with a friend Charles Sargent, but tactlessly showed Roosevelt the letter from Sargent complaining about it. However, after this unpromising start, the outdoor adventure went well.

'This is bully!' exclaimed Roosevelt as they camped

Theodore Roosevelt and John Muir at Glacier Point, Yosemite, 1903

under the stars at Bridalveil Meadow. 'This is the bulliest!' as the 70 year-old Muir pulled him out of a snowdrift.

'I never before had a more interesting, hearty, and manly companion,' Muir wrote.

But the president missed his wish for a politics-free weekend. Muir's message got through.

Lying out at night under those giant sequoias was lying in a temple built by no hand of man, a temple grander than any human architect could by any possibility build, and I hope for the preservation of the groves of giant trees simply because it would be a shame to our civilization to let them disappear. They are monuments in themselves.

Thanks to his fur-covered cuddly mascot (with its ultra-modern bendable limbs) Roosevelt achieved re-election in 1905. With Muir now lobbying by letter, Roosevelt went on to designate 230,000 square miles as National Forest—6 per cent of the land area of the USA—along with five National Parks and 23 National Monuments, including the Grand Canyon. And even today, the best bears wear Roosevelt-style eyeglasses. And they are called Theodore, please, not Edward.

In the last fifty years, roughly one third of the world's wild forest has been destroyed. The rate of destruction is itself speeding up, and if that trend continues, all the remaining wild trees will be gone within the lifetime of most of us.

Deforestation on its own extinguished the Easter Islanders and the ancient Mayan Civilisation.

In *Collapse,* Jared Diamond has listed, along with deforestation, another eleven ways—from overpopulation and toxic waste to global warming—in which we, the world civilisation, are damaging ourselves, and all twelve of which we have to stop, straight away. Thus implying that the world now needs a minimum of twelve activists, each equipped with blanket, small sack of flour, eagle-feather pen and a fluffy white beard…

In 1869, John Muir helped drive two thousand and fifty sheep into the high Sierras at the back of Tuolumne. And was able to see for himself how their little teeth nibbled any regenerating trees, shaved the yellow grasses and meadow herbs, and destroyed not just the forest but the soil itself (soil erosion is number two on Diamond's list).

See them, the 'hoofed locusts' as Muir came to call them, spreading contentedly across the wide clearing beside the Tyndall Creek. Between the high peaks of Mount Tyndall, the setting sun shines contentedly on the woolly backs. The shepherds look up the meadow to where the lad's got the fire going, good. At the creek crossing, the banks of shrubby manzanita are now broken to mud, and downstream the water runs brown. Down goes the Penstemmon, the Explorers Gentian, trampled by the little black hoof.

And one sheep on the flock's western edge spots a gap leading slantwise into the trees. She hesitates— and a second sheep (the others call her Ethel) notices her hesitation and hesitates too. The first sheep, 'Mavis' as it might be, feels the hesitation spreading back through the flock and takes a first step sideways. All at once it's not Mavis and Ethel, it's everybody. And the dough cakes are going to burn black before the shepherds make camp tonight.

Sheep are not human beings. You'll never hear a sheep go, 'Nothing I can do, not all on my own.' If all of us who say 'Nothing I can do, not on my own' actually did it, then we wouldn't be all on our own. If we set off like Ethel and Mavis bravely towards a better world, the others will follow along, because sheep may be sheep but people are too.

The other reason for not doing anything is that we can't do everything. If you're serious about saving the planet, then you'll switch off all your household appliances at the wall socket, tie a large boulder to yourself, and jump into a lake. Even then, you've polluted the lake.

It's not necessary to do everything. All that's needed is for everybody to do *something*. Don't tear out the central heating, but switch to a more efficient boiler. Don't give up the car, but get a smaller one, and use public transport even when it's inconvenient. We don't all have fluffy white beards and the ear of the American president. But the huge problems of the world become less huge when divided by the six billion of us. One small step for a sheep becomes a five-day adventure among the talus fields for the entire flock.

If present trends continue, the wild forest will vanish: but present trends don't absolutely have to continue. Just sometimes, human beings have managed to get together to do something sensible. We did, between 1959 and 1979, collectively conquer the smallpox virus. This time, the task is harder: for the disease we have to vaccinate the world against is—ourselves.

Trees and the wilderness are a place to start. Today, one quarter of the UK's timber sales are Forest Stewardship Council certified (independently verified as being sustainably logged). Twelve per cent of the world's forests are protected in national parks or similar reservations. Including the greater part of North America's ones. And that last part is largely down to one man: wee Johnnie Muir from Dunbar.

Notes and references

p 163 (epigraph) Robert Frost: 'The Road Not Taken'.

p163 (epigraph) Yosemite climbing pioneer Yvon Chouinard, in a *Sierra Magazine* interview.

p170 Roosevelt: speech at Sacramento, 1903.

John Muir as a boy: statue by Valentin I Znoba, Dunbar

Further Reading

John Muir: The Eight Wilderness–Discovery Books, ed Terry Gifford (Diadem/The Mountaineers Books, 1992). Includes eight of Muir's most popular books: *The Story of My Boyhood and Youth*, *A Thousand Mile Walk to the Gulf*, *My First Summer in the Sierra*, *The Mountains of California*, *Our National Parks*, *The Yosemite*, *Travels in Alaska* and *Steep Trails*. If you're going to read just one book by John Muir, make it *My First Summer in the Sierra*, cheaply published by Canongate (2007) with an introduction by Robert Macfarlane.

All Muir letters quoted here are from William Frederic Badè: *The Life and Letters of John Muir* (Houghton Mifflin, 1924), itself quoted in full, along with Muir's studies of glaciers and much else in *John Muir: His Life and Letters and Other Writings*, ed Terry Gifford (Bâton Wicks, 1996—currently out of print).

A brief, readable introduction to Muir's life is Cherry Good: *On the Trail of John Muir* (Luath, 2000).

The Sierra Club's John Muir Exhibit, with most of his writings and much else, is at www.sierraclub.org.

For walking the John Muir Trail, combine the excellent *John Muir Trail Map-Pack* from Tom Harrison Maps with *The John Muir Trail* by Alan Castle (Cicerone). Add R J Secor's *The High Sierra: Peaks, Passes and Trails* (Mountaineers Books) if you want to stray off the official JMT line.

The John Muir Way is marked on current OS maps.

The John Muir Birthplace Trust, Dunbar: www.jmbt.org.uk

The John Muir Trust: www.jmt.org.uk

Index